Music Therapy – Intimate Notes

Music Therapy

Intimate Notes

Mercédès Pavlicevic

Jessica Kingsley Publishers
London and Philadelphia

First published in the United Kingdom in 1999 by
Jessica Kingsley Publishers Ltd,
116 Pentonville Road,
London N1 9JB, England
and
325 Chestnut Street,
Philadelphia
PA 19106, USA.

www.jkp.com

© Copyright 1999 Mercédès Pavlicevic

Library of Congress Cataloging in Publication Data
Pavlicevic, Mercédès.
Music therapy -- intimate notes / Mercédès Pavlicevic.
p.   cm.
Includes bibliographical references (p. ****) and index.
ISBN 1 85302 691 3 (hb : alk. paper). -- ISBN 1 85302 692 1 (pb : alk. paper)
1. Music therapy--Case studies. 2. Music therapists--Biography.
I. Title.
ML3920. P229 1999
615.8'5154--dc21
98--45894
CIP
MN
British Library Cataloguing in Publication Data
Pavlicevic, Mercédès
Music therapy – intimate notes
1. Music therapy
I. Title
615.8'5154

ISBN 1 85302 692 1 pb
ISBN 1 85302 691 3 hb

Printed and Bound in Great Britain by
Athenaeum Press, Gateshead, Tyne and Wear

Contents

In Loving Memory of
Julienne Cartwright (1928–1998)
Friend, mentor, colleague and companion of the spirit

Acknowledgements

Nine music therapists generously gave of their time, their energy, their misgivings and uncertainties, to become part of this book. I warmly thank Catherine Durham, Jean Eisler, Claire Flower, Nigel Hartley, Claire Hobbs, Judith Nockolds, Catherine O'Leary, Nicky O'Neill and Oksana Zharinova for their trust and their stories.

I thank the Nordoff-Robbins Music Therapy Centre in London for their grant in support of this book, and Pauline Etkin in particular for allowing me to do the interviews during one of my all-too-brief (and always stimulating) teaching spells in London.

Finally I salute Jessica Kingsley: for her vision, her listening, and for daring, as a publisher, to remain in touch, in tune and independent.

Mercédès Pavlicevic
Johannesburg/London, December 1998

Some names have been changed to protect clients' identities and the privacy of their families.

Introduction
Finding our Muses

You walk into a room full of musical instruments, another person is there, greeting you and inviting you to choose an instrument. You pick up two sticks, one in each hand, approach something that looks like a glockenspiel marimba thing with lots of wooden bars, and give it a tap. Mmmmm, nice, so try another tap, also good, a bit more on the left then right, and it sort of sounds like – a tune… so you try tap the same again, but it doesn't quite work. Oh dear, you never could play, and this tune sounds like nonsense, but wait a minute, there is a drum! You walk over and – listen to that sound! Tap a bit more, a bit more, and the tune of 'twinkle twinkle little star' comes to your mind, you tap it out… you notice this other sound, with your sound somewhere on the right, and you don't quite know what it is doing and it isn't 'twinkle twinkle', but rather nice. You realize that the other person is playing something at the piano. She seems to know what she's doing, her music sounds nice, oh well – you're not pretending to be a musician in the first place, and 'twinkle twinkle' is a bit childish… so you'll just hit the drum a bit more… The drum gets louder and stronger and your beating draws you along before you know it, you are inside a big, big sound, all over the room! The piano also is in a big sound, and you hit harder and harder, start feeling excited, this is fast and loud and fun… even faster and louder, and suddenly you have this feeling of wanting to burst, burst into crying or is it laughing, and you can't stop this drumming. The drum sound is all inside you and you shake, you quiver, you break the speed-limit, there is colour some place on the left, you feel it down your back a bit, your body heats up around your tummy, and there seems to be some breeze on your neck, a dark maroon colour, moving around you … the colour starts to slow, get broader and spread, your tapping is quieter, slower, and you feel heavy, a bit slowed up after all that speeding, and then you realize you want to cry. Just quietly, a bit, your corner eye is damp, wet actually. You sniff, oh goodness, you're crying, you haven't for years, how embarrassing. There is silence in the room – and the heat around your tummy is still there. What happened? Where was all the sound, the noises, you can't quite remember, you have a feeling that there was something but you don't know what, and who is this person at the piano, anyway… she seems quite good at it.…

That was someone like you and I having some music therapy and probably not knowing what is going on: what is musical about it, what it is supposed to do, and why music therapy, anyway. But knowing there is a feeling about it, a colour, a heat, some 'thing' that seems to take over and make you feel feelings that were not there before. And then the feeling lingers.

So what does tapping a drum have to do with 'therapy'?

In this book you will read nine stories told me by nine music therapists. I interviewed each one, and each interview was moving, impassioned, complicated. Some interviews left me drained, others euphoric, some dissatisfied: had I grasped the story? What if I got it wrong – not just the story but the feeling of it, the space and pace of it, the sorrow, the loneliness, the passion and celebration of it? What if I transgressed some deeply intimate confidence? For the interviews, each one, were intimate. Each of the music therapists spoke about themselves, about their own lives in music and the music in their lives, about their work with clients/patients/persons in music therapy. Some cried remembering patients who had died; some laughed at themselves, at how unseeing they had been; some were softly reminiscent of work done long ago, alone in the dark, in the early days of the profession with no support, no supervision… with no one to tell stories to.

The music therapists that you will meet cover a range of ages and experience. I approached each on the basis that they had not written about music therapy, and my colleagues and I had heard them talk about their work at various presentations. Oksana Zharinova, in her early twenties and in her second year of training as a music therapist, first interviewed me thoroughly, asking me why had I chosen her, why would her story be useful, which bit should she tell me first, and how would I use it. While Jean Eisler, the most experienced of us all, told me her story of Wendy, a fiery passionate child, I listened to Jean's own life of passion, colour and suffering. Nigel Hartley I interviewed in a cluttered, cosy Porto cabin in the grounds of Sir Michael Sobell Hospice in Oxford, and he spoke with quiet elegance, reflective intensity, and constant self-questioning about life and death in hospice work. Claire Hobbs and I paused often to look at the daffodils in the garden and the lovely paintings in her home: we needed distractions from the bleak world of her work in a secure forensic unit in London. By the end of the interview with Cathy Durham in Bristol, I felt as though I had spent three hours trapped inside Shireen's body that could not move, could not see or hear, and that was intensely lonely and unfelt. As Claire Flower spoke of her work with Sinead, a physically handicapped child, Madeleine, her delicious one-and-a-half-year-old daughter, pinned me to her perfect self with her perfect eyes, so that for the first half-hour, the tape recorder listened and recorded our interview without me. Catherine O'Leary wrapped me in a blanket and made sure I was warm and comfortable, to absorb fully the complex work of Guided Imagery in Music, on a miserable damp foggy morning in Nottingham. Judith Nockolds and I sat on the floor, and her story of Jim was warm and moving – I was unsure, afterwards, whether I had asked the right questions: so complete was the music she played me. Nicky O'Neill's tale of Giorgos was slow and measured, and had me constantly interrupting, wanting to know more; we debated at length how to portray the tragedy and richness of his short life.

My role, throughout the interviews, has been one of a listening, questioning mind. Although the transcripts of the interviews needed careful sculpting into the shape of a story, I tried to interfere as little as possible with 'the voice' of each of the speakers. The stories are, as much as possible, in the form of an 'oral' text. The reflections in each story are my own.

This book does not attempt to portray all aspects of music therapy practice, nor is it an academic/theoretical text – hence the absence of bibliographical references. Further reading is listed at the end of the book. The text aims, rather, to fill a gap created by existing music therapy books that emphasize its theoretical/academic basis, and that may leave the lay reader somewhat puzzled as to what 'goes on' inside the music therapy room.

It has been an intimate privilege to enter into these stories, and I feel proud and humbled to be part of this complicated, inexact, exhilarating and most demanding profession. I warmly thank 'the nine' who shared with me their time, passions and exasperations. I hope that the stories, and the reflections on each, do tribute to their work, and to that of the wonderful persons – some deeply disabled – who have been their fellow travellers in music therapy. And in life.

PART I

Music Therapy with Children

CHAPTER I

Daniel
Blossoms and Baptism[1]

The end

Now, I am nearly at the end of my training as a music therapist, and looking back, I don't know how it happened that I am here – all the way from western Ukraine! I didn't know that I was going to be a music therapist, I wasn't dreaming of it… I never thought that this is what I am supposed to do. But what I do know is that I had that urge in me which said, 'what you are doing is not enough, something is there for you to do and you have to find it'. So I was looking for it and here I am.

In my second year with some of my adult clients, when they come to sessions and play, I hear myself playing music in a way that I would never play if I were playing on my own. They draw out of me the music which is inside me, for them. And I think, yes OK, by being who they are, they are making me listen, pulling music out of me, and an energy. But there is something more to it, more than using a technique or listening carefully, something greater, from up there. It is something which I don't consciously acknowledge, but which I am aware of existing in the work that we do. I know that such a tentative and accepting attitude to these external forces has something to do with my family tradition or maybe my culture… I know that I feel that it is coming from there – out, up there… but I don't want to scare it and to name it.…

1   Based on the interview with Oksana Zharinova. Oksana is in her final year of training at the Nordoff-Robbins Music Therapy Centre in London.

Sometimes, during the training, I have had a feeling that I am burning… as a fire… and sometimes now I have this feeling that I am giving so much energy, as if I am burning myself part by part, like a flower that loses its petals one by one. But I know that there is a rule in nature: if petals do not fall one by one, then the whole flower cannot open and it dies, falling off the stem without ever knowing or showing what was inside.

Daniel

Daniel was my first child as a student: my first client ever. It was last year. He was a six-year-old with cerebral palsy, learning difficulties, epilepsy and no speech. For the first session he came in a buggy and hardly moved. He wasn't really encouraged to move in his life, everything was done for him, everything was on his terms… I had a feeling that he could do things… although he was at a very low developmental level, under a year, probably. What I mean is, he would move his foot in the session, and we would put a tambourine in front of his foot, so that he could kick the tambourine and make a sound. He would stop immediately. Nothing was happening in the first three sessions. Either because I was a beginner – or else because nothing would happen. I felt bad, frustrated… first of all I *was* a student, he *was* my first child! We were supposed to do *something*, to develop, and I was so eager to apply my creativity and get something out of him! And after each supervision, I was told 'try playing less! Play less! Listen more, listen more!' And still it didn't help. You are there in the room wanting to give everything you have, knowing that this child can do something… because he can.

His parents brought Daniel to music therapy because they thought that this would help him to understand simple developmental tasks through concrete and direct activities. And also the experience of hearing himself being played by music, making him more aware of himself… because that is the first stage of personal development, when the child becomes aware of themselves and the other person there…. In the first few sessions he was emotionally detached, he didn't look at anyone, not at me, maybe he looked more at the co-therapist, my student-partner, because she was holding him. But she wasn't the musical source. Her role in the initial sessions was to hold him, although she did a lot more later on, encouraging him to use his hands, to play. He was very passive, both in and out of the music therapy room....

After the first session we decided to take him out of the buggy and either put him on the co-therapist's lap, or else on the floor on the mat. Also it was clear that it was difficult for him to respond to the piano, to make a connection with an unfamiliar sound coming from a 'big black box': it was something very distant as well... I was sitting up at the piano and he was down in his buggy. By session four, I had abandoned the piano completely and worked on the floor with him. As he started to utter occasional short vocal sounds – it was his first and only active musical contribution at the time – I was also vocalizing with him. I was singing a song, quite a structured song, and in the middle of it he started to vocalize more, extending the duration of his sounds – my voice could match every aspect of his vocal sounds: pitch, intensity and timbre. At first I was matching him completely, and then I started to extend a little bit what he was doing, still keeping very close to what he was doing... and then he started! He was just all over the place with his voice! Up and down, quiet and strong – it was really playful! Very imaginative! It felt very much like what I was doing with him was half because of what I was told in the training and half was completely intuitive.... I was listening and I knew that in order to establish contact with him I had to catch him... but at the same time, I don't know how to explain the timing of it, everything, it was complete intuition.... I knew that I had to match him, his voice, and at that particular moment, my voice *could* match his pitch and intensity and timbre.

While it was happening, I was amazed... first of all because it was the first time that I was completely with him... when I could experience him the way he was. It was very powerful – maybe because, well, if I'd had my own children, I probably would have experienced this quite differently – but I never had that experience. I was watching his breathing a lot... no he wasn't watching me at all... usually he sat with his eyes looking up at the ceiling. We didn't have any eye contact until session ten.

I had no sense that something like this was going to happen....

He had vocalized little bits in previous sessions, but it was two sounds here and two there... but here it was a continuous ten minutes... and not just vocalizing by himself in some way that was closed. It was a really open vocalization, related to what I was doing and very communicative... something big; sounds of incredible intensity and range. The more I did, the more he did... the vocalization fluctuated... it would come to something big and then go back, then come again....

It was coming from him – from the inside – from the whole of him – at that moment I had no question about this is *him* doing what *he* wants to do – it was very authentic – that is why it was so powerful and meaningful. His voice was really... something... and this was not a developmental thing....

What we were doing with his body in music therapy was trying to make him more aware of it. He always sat in a closed posture, with his hands bent at his chest. And although we were working with him as a whole, it still felt that when the voice came that here was something very very special.... it was like a vision... he revealed that he can do something – OK, I knew it, but it had stayed at the level of my 'knowing' and 'believing', not more than that... and finally here was the music child, which is ready to blossom! He showed that he's got that within him, which can sound and which is ready to communicate, given the right circumstances.

The vocalization finished and then nothing really happened afterwards... well, nothing had to happen afterwards. It was enough!

After this, I didn't have any more problems with thinking 'oh I can't do anything...'. Daniel helped me to believe that the contact is possible: forget about the dynamics of being a student, or even of being a therapist. I knew, after this, that contact was possible with him, I knew which way to go – and I also knew that if it is possible this way with him, then it will be possible another way... and also with other clients.

I was warned that after this I would want it to happen again... and don't, because this wish can destroy everything I do! I might end up frustrated after each session because it didn't happen again.... Well, in life things happen and they've gone but you keep them in your mind. Your experience becomes part of you, your life, even if you are not consciously aware of it. But because of these experiences, you are not the same anymore. So it didn't matter that this vocalization, with such intensity, didn't happen again…. The fact that it happened once gave me strength to do other things. The importance of that particular moment was that I got to know him! It completely changed the way that I looked at him afterwards. I started to believe in his ability and it enabled me – and I think him as well – to achieve further results in therapy. The co-therapist described that moment as being so still, she was afraid to breathe… and that particular session was the only one which wasn't videoed! And maybe it happened because it wasn't videoed….

Then a lot of things happened in our work together. He got much more active… he vocalized a lot afterwards, but never with such concentration of expression in terms of time and intensity. Also I could start to be more relaxed! I took that vocalization *so* seriously! And then, three or four sessions later, I realized that he needed something playful, and we did lots of shaker, tambourine and piano sound anticipation – like peek-a-boo games. Mother–baby type interactions, captivating musical activities, lots of contrast in the music to get his attention, lots of lively sounds and facial expressions from me and the co-therapist – to keep his attention going – and there were moments of musical connection here and there. When I took him in my arms, he would move and I would sing with his movements. He was very aware and then he began to look at me properly.

At the end he was much more independent and he knew… what was happening, he was much more aware. For a child with that low level of awareness, who comes to music therapy once a week, it is important to get used to a routine – we had twenty-five to thirty minutes every week. His mother felt that he was doing very well, he was starting to be much more aware of parts of his body because we did work with that, singing about different parts of his body or about the activities he did with his hands and feet. She was very happy about us concentrating on his drum beating, because at home he started to use his hands in useful and constructive ways. And we were encouraging this in music therapy. Having music working for us and believing in him we achieved a lot.

We had twenty-one sessions altogether… he was my first hands-on experience of music therapy.

Reflections

On 'doing' nothing

Infuriatingly, Daniel does nothing. Oksana knows that he can 'do', but he remains passive, looking at the ceiling, arms stiffly folded to his chest, apparently closed to her, to the co-therapist, and to the work. She has little sense of him. How do you respond to a child who does 'nothing'? The void that he presents, and his absence from the music therapy room, challenges a deeply natural aspect of human communication: that for communication to happen between people, we *need* the responsiveness of another person, we need them to *show* their responsiveness, whether in speech, movements or facial expressions, and we ourselves need to have a sense of *their* sensitivity to our influence – to mutual influence. We cannot communicate with someone who does not show any signs of being susceptible to us, influenced by us; who appears vacant.

Communication between Oksana and Daniel is a two-way process: Daniel begins to vocalize and at first he makes occasional short sounds. Oksana vocalizes too, but not just in any way: she listens to the quality of his voice, how short the sounds are, how high or low they are, whether she can hear any rhythm, any shape in what he does. And she adapts her own vocalizing in a way that is related to him, to his sounds. This is the beginning of interpersonal influence. She is influenced by what he does and by how he does it – no matter how tiny and apparently haphazard his sounds are at first – and her sensitivity to him sounds in her voice. He hears this, and feels her awareness of him in the song that she is singing, and in session four, this triggers something in him. Suddenly, he begins to vocalize much more intensely: he makes longer sounds, and immediately she responds, matching his longer, more intense sounds. In these moments, Oksana and Daniel connect with one another in a way that they have not been able to until now. What is interesting here, though, is that Oksana does more than just match, or mirror what he does. She begins to *extend* what he does.

This is crucial: in order for Daniel to extend himself, to grow, to develop, he needs to be shown where he can go with his voice. Now that he and Oksana have 'met', now that each has a sense of the other, through their vocalizing together, Oksana keeps close to what Daniel is doing: she continues to match his singing closely. In this way, he knows – he has a sense – that her singing is related to his. And when she does a bit more – sings for longer, or louder, or quicker – he then hears where he needs to go in order to remain connected to her. These subtle inter-timings happen at a micro level, which many of us are not aware of – but we all do it, whether we communicate with adults or with children: we tune into the speed, the loudness, the kind of sound that a person makes when they speak, move or gesture to us, and we are influenced by this. In order to communicate with another person, we change, we adapt, we shift towards them: we coordinate ourselves, our sounds, our movements, in order to let them know that we are present, interpersonally, and that we can *together* create meaning. In music therapy, this happens through music.

This shared meaning does not need to be verbal – it may not even be 'musical' in the formal sense. Rather, through creating sound-form with one another, Daniel and Oksana together enter into emotional meaning that is exclusive to them: to who each of them is, and to each of them in relation to one another. The meaning that they create together is not only about music: it is about one person getting to know another, and letting them know it. For Daniel, a child who appears passive, this cannot be a common experience.

It is the moment of change from his being passive to becoming active that gives Oksana a cue as to Daniel's 'music child'. The concept of the 'music child' (also known as the 'music person') was developed by Paul Nordoff and Clive Robbins: they speak of the 'music child' being the inner core of every human being, no matter how disabled, disturbed, or unwell. This inner core remains healthy and creative, and is the source of 'wellness' that music therapy taps. As we shall see in other stories, the 'music person' first needs to be found – and this is one of the skills of the music therapist: to elicit it, to call it forth, to engage with the part of the child (or adult) that remains well, despite the challenges and crises of life. Oksana has an instant sense of Daniel's music child, at that moment, and knows that, from now on, she 'knows' him. She speaks of his sounds as being authentic, as coming from the whole of him – not only from his 'disabled' self. This is the first time he reveals himself to her, and it releases something in him too. He becomes more active in later sessions, and his mother notices changes at home.

This story reveals a baptism; an induction, a beginning for them both. Oksana, a student in her first year of training, ready to apply her knowledge and creativity, and Daniel, ready to blossom, ready to begin, if only she can 'catch him'. Daniel allows her to.

CHAPTER 2

Wendy
'I Used To Be Crying Every Day...'[1]

The beginning (i)

Wendy came to the psychiatric ward of the hospital because she was beyond parental control. She'd never felt loved, her mother hadn't wanted her, she'd only just survived the first year of her life, had been in and out of hospital for failure to thrive and bruises... there was a complicated family history of changing partners and divorces. At the age of seven, she'd literally been shoved out by her mother and told to go and find her real father. Mother was already living with someone else. Father lived some houses down the road in a one-room attic. He was a part-time worker with little money and he now had to take in Wendy and her sister.

As a toddler Wendy had been to two or three nursery schools, and was very difficult: always in tantrums or tears, severely enuretic, forever trying to do things that never quite succeeded. When she started school she couldn't concentrate, was totally obsessed with why Mother didn't love her or want her. It seemed to her to be her fault and she was thoroughly miserable. She kept running away from school, and by nine years, could barely write her name or count to seven, she'd no idea of time, days, weeks or months. It was a total muddle in her head. Social Services asked the hospital to take her in while they tried to re-house her, her father and older sister, and provide backup support.

1   Based on the interview with Jean Eisler. Jean works at the Nordoff-Robbins Centre in London with children who have a range of needs.

A week after coming into hospital she was referred for music therapy. She came to the music therapy room for the first time, immediately chose the biggest drum and started some erratic drum-beating. I improvised at the piano, trying to meet her strong unsteady playing, and within a minute or two she was able to hold a regular beat. She was almost breathless with excitement. I said 'oh, it is so exciting' – as if to express her feeling – and we were off, getting faster, getting slower, in communication with one another. She was 'in balance'!

My intuitive feeling was that this was one of the first moments she had felt held – the steadiness of the piano rhythm held her, she could go with the music; the music went where she wanted. Finally she came to the piano, sat beside me at the treble end as I improvised simply and quietly. She just played one note and the next beside it with two fingers. Gradually she moved to another note and then another, and within a few moments she was all over the piano…. I started to put together the bits she was speaking and singing at the piano, and we turned this into a goodbye song. In the end she was all over the keyboard with lovely rhythmic playing with her two fingers… taking it all in while I sang. A lively, instinctively dramatic child!

The beginning (ii)

A few years after the death of my husband in 1966 in an alpine storm, when my two sons had completed their college education and were both working, I returned to Britain. I'd spent twenty-five years in Prague, and was hoping to find some form of work, maybe in the music world, teaching. Within six weeks of returning, I came across the book *Therapy in Music for the Handicapped Child* by Paul Nordoff and Clive Robbins, and that was it! I trained as a music therapist in 1974. It was the first comprehensive course given by Paul Nordoff and Clive Robbins at Goldie Leigh hospital in London. Everything about the training excited me – so many things fell into place! The idea that you could use music in this way, that you could reach people through musical improvisation, that this improvisation reflected one's true nature and formed a direct means of communication…. I had a handicapped niece, but other than that I'd had no contact with handicapped people..

My life experiences in Prague were of being foreign, an outsider… then there were the very difficult times in the 1950s, when Pavel, my husband, was considered a dissident. A number of friends had lost their husbands: either executed or life imprisonment following the horrendous political trials of the early 1950s. One helped where one could. But Pavel was out of work for several years, and we had our own children to bring up – and so on. So it was the 'have-nots' helping the 'have-nots', and it greatly strengthened one's emotional awareness of, and links with, one's fellow beings. It also gave me a strong feeling for the 'under-people'. I now had a very instinctive feel for the handicapped, the hurt people, the lonely and the disturbed – and suddenly, here was Paul Nordoff meeting people like this through music! I needed to absorb his ideas as to how you might go about working with music, and I immediately began reading Jung and other important writers on personal psychological development. In Prague there had been no books on psychiatry: Freud, Jung and others had hardly been translated and were almost taboo, so I was very ignorant. This again opened my eyes to possibilities in my own life! Many things came together, and it was very exciting – talk about the third phase in your life: I was fifty-six at the time!

Wendy

I'd been working as a music therapist for ten years when Wendy came along – ten very groping years with not much guidance, because we didn't have anyone more senior to turn to for supervision in those days. The clinical awareness just had to grow in oneself after the training. I'd been working with autistic children – but here was a child who wasn't autistic, who had these immense emotional problems to work with…. She came at a very good moment for me, because I'd had experience of helping many severely multiply handicapped children find self-expression through music – and some of the autistic children had become very expressive in their music… but she was the first from a child psychiatry in-patient ward… and what a child!

Wendy looked like a small Victorian waif – skinny, pale, undersized, her clothes hung on her – they probably mostly belonged to her older sister. She'd sometimes come in wearing a pair of grown-up court shoes, much too big for her, acting the big girl. Mousy hair... not a striking looking child, really waif-like. Sometimes a friend on the ward would lend her a sweater because she hadn't got any proper warm clothes.

I saw her weekly, and we worked together for nine months. She was an incredibly alive little girl, and what astounded me was that this alert child with all this capability was, in scholastic terms, so incapable. All this gradually emerged in our work: she would try and act the leader and imitate things she saw on telly. 'This is Music Time!... This is an instrument, it is made of wood, it costs a lot of money, it costs five pounds, it was made five thousand years ago...'. None of it made sense, really.... On the other hand, she had an incredibly strong sense of how to hold on, to keep herself together. She was totally disturbed by this feeling of not being able, and therefore, loveless – yet deep inside, I think she sensed her own strength. By the third session, I was playing a lullaby kind of music and she was doodling in her mind, her words were only just audible: 'I can play the piano, I can play... when I was new I couldn't play, when I was two I played the piano, when I was three I played to my mum, if I'd played, you would have loved me...'. It was absolutely linked with the need for 'I can do it' and 'you would have loved' ... this little person that I am, playing and achieving. She got the feeling of, 'I am a person' and 'I can'. Our songs became filled with 'I can... play the piano, beat the drum... do this, do that...'. Gradually, through the months, all the hurt began to come out. Her voice began to grow.

To begin with she had a tiny low singing voice.... As our work together developed, her breath control expanded, and her melodic phrases became longer and longer. Her voice – her singing – enabled her to express herself, to express things in her life more and more fully and expansively, now and again through long, long arias. We had started our work in the autumn, and by Christmas she wanted to have all the Christmas carols about mother and baby, and to learn to understand the words, for example, 'what's a manger?' – things she'd sung but never understood. Then she really began to take off, to act out and be the omnipotent teacher, TV personality or pop-star: that was when her emotional life became so clear to me. She'd start a fairy tale of some kind and it would become her story: two little children, going out and being lost... which is exactly what had happened to her and her sister, of course. She would act it, sing it – and would tell me when to play or not, and I would just act/play/sing what I thought she wanted. Or else she would say 'stop' and begin something different – when certain trains of thought were too painful... At other times, she might address an imaginary crowd of children and start talking or singing to them. She would get so involved in this, in herself, that the children would disappear and the music become stronger, more prominent in its own right....

She would begin singing and talking about various things and events in her own life. Not necessarily directly to me but out loud instead of just talking in her head... which she'd been doing for years because she'd been so miserable – so alone and no one listened. Anyway, she began to sing these things out loud. The speaking of it and knowing that it was out into the world helped her to get it all out, to re-organize it, to re-create it, if you like. She found that it was OK to do this, and it was important that the music held it all: held her talking, singing, acting in sounds. I would improvise at the piano, offering music that matched and met her mood, the mood of her stories, her talking, her emotional timbre. The music could – and had to – meet her movements, their tempo and phrasing. By playing freely and spontaneously, I could support what she did, sang, acted. And make it bearable for her. She recognized this support; she recognized that she could be part of the music, could enter into it and shape it as she wanted, because I was there to do just that, with her and she felt good and whole.

For example, in one session, there were three reed horns. She came in – she was acting out all sorts of stories by now – she picked up the horns, blew them and said 'these are the three ones' – blew one 'that's the daddy one' – blew another and said 'that's the mu-' and stopped because there wasn't a mummy. She went on to sing out loud, 'and the mummy one wasn't there, it was very sad'. At that point I could come in with the sort of music that was not obtrusive, but that held the atmosphere. She was finally able to say '... and the mummy one, they didn't know, but she was under the grass...'. She in fact buried her mother out of the story.... I don't think she could have spoken like that without music; without the holding feel that there was. The music meant that it was not just her speech, alone, which could be so naked. She sensed that the musical atmosphere was totally involved in what she was saying about her mother. The atmosphere held her in such a way that she was able to carry through and carry on, expand her story into music, knowing that the music could allow this, could support it and contain it. She could say all these things – sing them if she wanted to. The music could move slowly, quietly, atmospherically for her.

I sensed right away this feeling of what it was like not to have felt loved, to have felt not wanted.... I'd had a lot of times as a child when I didn't talk... because I was the middle one of a big family and easily felt lost and snubbed. I also think that my experiences in the 1950s in Prague were very intense and I was very aware of us – Pavel and I, our family – not being wanted. When I first arrived there from Britain, I wasn't able to speak Czech, and didn't become fluent for two or three years. So often, things didn't make sense.... There are so many things in one's own life that you don't think about in the music therapy session, but it all somehow echoes intuitively. That is why and how you can meet the child with all your own life experiences... my life and hers.

Wendy led our sessions absolutely, and I knew she was going to lead as soon as she felt the necessary security. She felt the strength of the music in relation to what she did... the music was always there for her, it resonated with her, and she with the music. There were other times when she'd say 'Stop!' and then act some alarming big story and I wasn't to play. But somehow I could usually creep in and the music would hold it.... We used all different kinds of music... sometimes I would have to improvise nursery rhymes or kiddy streetwise stuff, sometimes the music was quite atonal, sometimes very thin. At other times it was great big music to match the terrific energy and speed of her drumming. Sometimes it was a mess. Sometimes she'd break off and move to something totally different – it was quite difficult when she broke off and I was left in the middle, not knowing where to go. But I knew there were so many things going on in her mind at the same time – and perhaps there was something stronger and more urgent than what we were actually doing – or possibly the music that I was improvising wasn't quite strong enough or suitable for that particular moment....

There were moments in music therapy when she blossomed and her voice really came through: she totally accepted that this was an atmosphere and a place where she could really be all these things that were within her. I don't think this was a conscious knowledge. All sorts of things could happen in music, but I don't think she was fully aware of what was really happening until later. She developed and changed so fast during our time together, finding expression for all the things that she'd been holding inside herself with tremendous frustration all those years. These could now find tremendously strong expression in music. And her experience was made that much stronger by the fact that I had the range of the piano to improvise on. This was a child who needed the strength of the piano: the harmonies and dynamics, at times, had to be colossal and they varied a lot! I was playing totally instinctively, I was intuitively led... we did not sing many songs exactly, but the music usually had a pattern, a structure that could enclose things, draw them out, hold them still, give them full vent.... She would burst in and you'd have to burst right in there too, with her, wherever she was. At the end of the sessions, though, there was always enclosing music. Particularly in one session when some of the really harsh things that had happened in her life emerged. She was almost beside herself with it – she just couldn't sing anymore and had burst into a sort of can-can dance all the way round and round the room to let off this enormous energy and frustration that was there. I had to meet this energy through music, but eventually I had to help her to bring it down. So this time we brought it down together, to a calm goodbye song which she finally managed to sing very reflectively and softly... then she went out, whistling a little snatch of a song. I think it may have reflected her sense of relief, or happiness even.

What she demanded of me was very good for me – and for my development as a therapist! I had to find the freedom to improvise really genuinely – I had to be there, I couldn't think or rationalize, 'I'll do this or that'. I had to be there, in the moment, and draw on whatever resources I had there and then. She never used my name and rarely looked at me when we were playing. I was part of the music room...

there wasn't a personal thing, not a personal relationship. It was a musical relationship – yet it wasn't impersonal... I was the music person – I was not the 'Jean' person. With her it really was therapy in the music – music therapy – therapy *through* the music! The music had to have incredible variety, had to reflect the variety of her world. She had a very direct musical line, which came straight out of her feelings – uncluttered, very free. When she was really in the flow of things, then everything made total sense. She was absolutely clear about feelings. But all the rest, what the world was about, that was just a jumble – which she would have to sort out.

About halfway through our work, I played some of the tapes to the ward staff, who'd been asking, 'what's going on in music?' – they couldn't believe that she had this huge expressive voice right deep inside her.... She was also now having group sessions with other children, and was beginning to be able to hold her own. She also had individual play therapy. About halfway through our work, when she was revealing so many things through our music, the play therapist said to our team, 'I think it will be a long time before Wendy comes out with any of the real story...'. And here she was coming out with it in the music sessions!

In the hospital there was a small psychiatric school unit with almost one-to-one attention. Within six months of our work together commencing, she was beginning to be able to do tasks – because she wasn't having disturbing thoughts going round in her mind all the time without an outlet. By about eight months she was able to sit and learn, and by nine months she was to leave the hospital and would be going to a new day school. The family had been re-housed.

Wendy came running into her session one morning – it was our thirty-fourth session. She knew she was leaving. They'd given her a watch. She showed it to me and asked me to set the time. I said 'it's half-past eleven' and set it for her. She burst into song and drumming– 'I can sing now, I can play the piano, I can do everything, I can tell the time now, and it is half-past eleven...' all the things that she could do. Suddenly she stopped dramatically and sang – 'I used to be crying every day, every day... and I can... not have to cry... any any any more'. We created the most amazing aria together: 'I can't cry anymore, I don't have to cry anymore, I'm getting so very very big, I don't have to cry anymore'. She was tiny of course… but she was totally sure that she was going to be all right. And then we finished. She said, 'Stop when I click my fingers, like this!' And a few moments later, she clicked and we stopped. She added jauntily, 'That was good, wasn't it?' and we said goodbye and that was it.

She went off to a very good school near where she was living – and within a year went up from one class to the next – she was gradually catching up with her physical and intellectual age group. But as she was such a lively spark, by the time she was fourteen, fifteen, Social Services were worried about her living with a rather elderly father and an older sister who was already going out with boys. So they sent her to a boarding school in the country, which turned out to be excellent. She'd come home for the holidays…. She'd also come back to the hospital every now and then to see her friends and was fine!

What a gift, this child! To work with a child who was such a convincing demonstration of everything Paul Nordoff ever said about the music child being there – ready to be given a chance to flourish and take with it all the hurt feelings and everything else as well. Music felt so strong to her, and was so strong within her; music felt safe, she could rely on it, she could be part of transforming it while transforming herself.

All this work took place in a portakabin out in the woods in the hospital grounds. We had a grand piano! It was a wonderful place, quite separate from anything else. It was the music house – there was nobody else nearby. In the winter it could even be covered in snow… it was about two hundred yards from the ward. The children would come over… they would be brought to the first session or two, and then would come on their own, and the door led straight into the music room. We had curtains on the windows so that people couldn't look in… it was warm – it was its own place, just right… two or three drums, conga, xylophone, and so on, and a microphone…. I don't think Wendy knew that everything was being recorded, but I am thankful it was, because a lot of her words were expressed very softly, as though she was burbling to herself. I couldn't always gather what she was saying while we played together. What was important, though, was that this was being said out loud, listened to and acknowledged. I could decipher it later.

Over the years music has become a new kind of language for me, for my feelings, my musical awareness. I had a very rich musical background from which to draw, but it was very much based in the music of the past and of the time in which I grew up. My musical roots are grounded in classical and English church music. At home, we were a large family: we made music together, we sang madrigals, played quartets. I played professionally in chamber orchestras, mostly Bach, other Baroque music, and English composers up to the 1940s. Then I left the UK with my husband to live in Prague for twenty-five years – in a very frustrated musical and tough political environment. Fortunately one's musical roots cannot be taken away and they provided a good foundation for music therapy. I am not a great modern atonal player, and I had to work hard to develop creative flexibility.

Of course I also gained a feeling of self-assurance from working with Wendy – and with the other children who came my way – when I realized that I could meet and really help them through music-making together. I was very lucky... first of all to have been a student on that first Nordoff-Robbins music therapy training course, and then to have been faced with a child like Wendy.... But then Paul Nordoff often said, 'you always get the child you need!' And I got her. All her needs and also her immense inner strength.

Reflections

Keeping the Beat

One of the first things Jean says about Wendy's first music therapy session is that her beating on the drum is erratic – and that within minutes, Wendy is able to hold a regular beat. What is the significance of beating in music therapy? Why is Jean keen to get Wendy's beat to become regular?

In their pioneering work with handicapped children, Paul Nordoff and Clive Robbins noticed that the drum, a primitive, noisy, almost barbaric instrument, reveals the child's expression directly and simply, allowing the child to sound themselves in a way that says, 'this is me, here I am', without the complications of melody and harmony. Wendy's beating is heard by her therapist as an expression – a direct expression – of who Wendy is. Wendy's world is out of control, lacks predictability, lacks constant love and care: she is a battered child, has changed several nursery schools, and finally has been thrown out of home. Her drum beating – erratic and disorganized – communicates to Jean something about Wendy's inner world: the world of her psyche, the extent of disorganization in her emotional life.

However, we need to be careful not to explain Wendy's erratic beating as only portraying 'negative' aspects of her inner life. We also need to listen to the energy of her beating. Somewhere in the erratic disorder there is undoubtedly a buoyancy, a playfulness, an alertness and animation, a freedom of expression, and an intensity of commitment to beating the drum. Jean hears these 'positive' aspects of Wendy's beating *at the same time* as she hears the disorder and erratic qualities – even if these 'positive' aspects are latent, rather than overt. She hears Wendy's potential for rhythmic flexibility, and her response is to almost immediately provide an opportunity for Wendy to steady her beat.

How does Jean do this? Imagine Wendy playing the drum, all over the place, probably quite loudly, and Jean is at the piano, listening intently to Wendy's rhythms, speed and loudness. Jean hears little shape and rhythmic steadiness – so how can she begin to join in at the piano, with drumming that is quite so disorganized? One of the things that Jean does is to listen to *some aspect* of Wendy's playing – let's say that amidst all the erratic drum-beating, Wendy gives three beats that are more or less steady. Jean hears these, and with spilt-second timing, reproduces them on the piano. Jean keeps going, repeating Wendy's three steady beats, and offering Wendy a regular pulse. This moment is critical: the regular beat is not imposed by Jean on to their joint playing. Jean has got the quality of the pulse, in the first place, from Wendy's drumming. Critically, though, she instantly hears its potential for becoming a *basic beat*: a beat that can eventually be shared between them, a beat that belongs to them both.

Let's think a bit more about this micro-exchange and adaptation of timing. It is incredibly difficult to play 'out of beat', or 'out of time' with someone: we all have a biological tendency to 'fit in' with the rhythm and tempo and phrasing of the world around us (which psychologists call 'entrainment'). One of the skills of music therapists is to counter this 'natural' tendency when and if necessary. Thus, Jean has to be able to keep steady in her playing, resisting the natural tendency to join Wendy's unsteady playing, while at the same time, 'tuning in' to Wendy's (erratic) drumming. Critically, Jean's steady playing must continue to relate to Wendy's drumming: her steadiness is a *related* steadiness; its flexibility must enable Wendy to sense Jean's piano playing as being related to her own drumming, even though her drumming may be all over the place.

Within moments, Wendy's playing steadies – and this is an intuitive, responsive steadying – and Jean and Wendy share the beat. Together they play the *basic beat*. This provides a meeting ground: the basic beat is predictable, it has a serenity and supportiveness that can hold both Wendy and Jean together in the music; the music being created by them concurrently. Jean constantly listens to Wendy's beating and continues to travel with it in her own spontaneous playing at the piano. By sharing the beat within minutes of their first session, they lay a foundation for the nine months of music therapy work together.

This is a description of the music itself. But this description does not begin to address the various and complex layers of meaning in these music therapy sessions.

Re-creating the world

Wendy expresses the events of her life through singing: singing freely, making up as she goes along, re-telling events, using fairy tales and Christmas stories to rearrange the persons in her life: her mum who doesn't love her, her father with whom she lives, the dreadful things that have happened to her. This rearranging and 'expelling' in music therapy is in part a *catharsis*, a release of pent-up energy and emotion which Wendy has had to hold in, at great personal cost. Children who are traumatized and who have no opportunity to 'work through' things that have happened to them (i.e., to express, rearrange and expel them), can become distracted, 'badly behaved', irritable, unable to sleep – they begin to behave in a 'disturbed' manner.

Something more than a catharsis happens in the sessions. Wendy re-creates her life. She re-visits painful events that have been blocked out, forgotten, kept aside, too traumatic to recall. Music therapy helps Wendy to 'take control' of these events by first, daring to look at them again – this child has a courageous spirit – and then, in the sessions, by infusing them with new colours, new harmonies and emotional textures. By re-telling the stories of her life, by having Jean listen and accompany her re-telling, by being permitted to take the stories to their extreme depths, horizons, and by daring to become the stories in song and dance and drum-playing, Wendy engages in a profound act of re-creating her life, with all its tempests and tears.

In the music-making, Jean picks up not only the physical/musical qualities of Wendy's movements and playing, but also their colour, their texture, their 'feeling', and these Jean presents to Wendy, through music. How can music portray, reflect, imitate, present the 'feeling' dimensions of our lives?

Life in music

We all know, intuitively perhaps, that music is much more than just sounds put together, or pretty tunes. Music makes us *feel*: high, low, slow, speeded up – we recognize our own feelings in music and we respond to music with feeling. Some music 'sounds sad', we say – but how do we know? Where is the feeling of sadness – is it *really* in the music? Or is it in us – and if it is in us, then why do we say that it is *the music* that sounds sad (or joyful or angry or whatever)?

Composers, philosophers and psychologists talk about music portraying the very qualities of our emotional lives: the essential qualities of who we are. We recognize these qualities and respond to them when we listen to music, which is why it is so powerfully significant to many of us (whether we are 'musical' or not). For example, our essential self may – at different times – be vivacious/limpid, rough/smooth, cloying/darting, strong/brittle, expansive/narrow. These essential qualities underpin our feeling lives as well as our ways of expressing ourselves and relating to others. Thus, our sorrow may be a rough, tempestuous, strong sorrow, expressed through movements and sounds with those very qualities: our movements, voices, gestures, acts will be rough tempestuous and strong. Someone else might express sorrow in a way that is brittle and dispersed, with corresponding acts, gestures and vocal sounds. In other words, how we express ourselves – and how we express any of our many feelings – depends on who we are and how we are essentially. Wendy is a tempestuous, explosive child, full of vitality and fury: her vitality and explosiveness are qualities that feature in *both* her rages and in her joyful excitements. In her music, Jean uses the range and depth of the piano in order to resonate with these very qualities that are essential to Wendy: tempestuous, explosive and furious music. This is the music that Wendy needs to be part of. Wendy recognizes Jean's music as being *her* own music, Jean is not 'just making it up' – not at all! Jean 'tunes in' to Wendy constantly, listening to her drumming, her dancing, her singing, and providing spontaneous songs and music that meet and colour and absorb Wendy's pain and strength. Wendy leads Jean, she 'knows' what she needs to do, although perhaps not verbally, rationally or even consciously; and she also trusts that Jean is there with her.

What if Jean gets it wrong? What if this fury and vitality are all in Jean's musical imagination? Imagine the following scene: you, the reader, are absolutely full of energy and feeling, you are beating a drum with splendid noise, and the therapist at the piano plays quietly and soothingly, in order to 'calm you down'. Well, the first question is, why be calmed down? If you are full of loudness, then, damn it, that is what you are, in that moment, and want to be, and how you want to play. You do not need to be soothed or calmed right this minute, thank you. And what happens here is that the therapist's 'efforts' to calm you down will, very likely, provoke you to even greater energy and loudness. So what you need is the therapist to be *with you* in the flow and strength and power of your feeling as you express these on the drum or marimba or in your singing, or whatever. In this way, you experience your feeling as being shared. *Somebody* knows how you feel, somebody has a sense of the very essence of who you are – and lets you know it! You experience this knowing, this being known by another, directly in your joint music-making. The music validates, affirms how you feel and who you are. By 'trying' to 'calm you', the therapist is not validating or meeting you: she is, in effect, saying, 'don't be like that, be like this...'.

If Jean's music were inappropriate, then Wendy would not 'tune into' it, would not respond to it, and the music would not hold and contain this volcanic child. Jean and Wendy would not connect. There is a beautiful moment in Jean's story, when she describes the end of a session that is especially passionate, enabling Wendy to give full vent to her feelings, and then, through their joint playing, Jean *and* Wendy 'bring it down' *together*. They end the session with a calm, tender goodbye. This final scenario is a powerful statement of the quality of their commitment to their work. Wendy allows Jean to lead her towards tenderness and quiet – she knows that Jean has been with her through her tempests and tantrums, and will hold her now, in the music, in this quiet ending.

Jean's acknowledgement of what Wendy has given her, as a human being and as a music therapist, is a testimony to her own humility, strength, imagination, and passion for the work. It is also a testimony to joint journeyings in music therapy. As music therapists we learn, we are grown, we are 'musicked' through encounters with the very old and very young, the very frail and very complex, and the immensely powerful human beings with whom we enter into music.

CHAPTER 3

Sinead

'Here is my Arm…'[1]

The setting (i)

Madeleine, who is one and a half, listened to the first half-hour of this interview with large open blue eyes pinned on me. While Claire, her mother, talked about her work with Sinead,[2] a deeply handicapped child, Madeleine munched a biscuit, drank juice, burped, cooed, banged her bottle on the table, and never once allowed me to remove myself from her gaze.

Having had my own two children during this time of being a music therapist means that I see and experience all the stages of human development instantly, directly. They are not in a textbook, but right here, and I see how everything is so linked: the physical development, the cognitive, the emotional – all are connected. And having to manage or contain the whole gamut of emotions that my children have, that they trigger in me and that I have to bear – the rage and the love, swinging wildly at times between them.…

Going back to work, after our two-year-old had dealt with the new baby sister, I was working with a disturbed boy who was physically threatening. I felt so much stronger with him than I had done before

1   Based on the interview with Claire Flower. Claire is involved in training music therapy students at the Guildhall School of Music, and at the Nordoff-Robbins Music Therapy Centre, both in London.

2   Sinead's name has not been changed, in accordance with the wishes of her family.

having children... and it wasn't to do with being physically in a better position to deal with him. It was because I had survived the onslaught from a two-year-old and I knew there was a certain strength in me that could manage that. And if I could manage that, then things being hurled at me across the room weren't so bad. And, actually, with him it wasn't just a physical attack, it was a whole emotional attack as well....

The setting (ii)

The school is very small one: at the moment it has about twenty-five children right across the range of special needs – children with physical disabilities, severe and moderate learning difficulties, with autism, with emotional disturbance, and with language and communication disorders. It feels as though the school takes children whose other schools have not worked out, whose parents are having trouble finding a school that suits them, or whose placements have broken down. The school was set up by a couple in their home over thirty years ago, and has grown from there. When I started working there about six years ago, I hadn't worked with that age group of children at all – four- to twelve-year-olds – and it took me ages to settle. It is very much a family school, and like every family, it has wonderful and difficult aspects!

There is a lot of good work done with the children. The school is ridiculously small, physically small – there are four classes – and there is always lots of music going on: piano music and singing and playing. This is great on one hand, but there is never quiet, silence... and the music therapy room is right in the middle of all this!

Sinead: The trio

I started working with Sinead after I had been there for a year. She was then nearly six, and was in the class for the children with more physical disabilities. Molly, her class teacher, felt that Sinead was getting increasingly frustrated at not being able to communicate. Molly felt that she understood a lot, made sense of everything going on around her, and was getting upset and becoming quite withdrawn. That was the referral... the whole system is *ad hoc* because the place is so small.

Sinead was brain damaged at birth, and has cerebral palsy. She is bright and completely knobbled physically. She is in a wheelchair, has very little use of arms and fingers, poor head control, poor eye control – and she has no verbal expression of her own.

When I started to see Sinead in music therapy, I worked together with Sarah, the speech therapist. We felt that Sarah could help to facilitate movement, help her access some of the instruments, and would understand Sinead and her attempts at communicating a bit more than I did. It was an absolute disaster.... I was worried of what Sarah was going to make of music therapy: she hadn't worked with a music therapist before, I hadn't worked with a speech therapist before, and we launched in without thinking about any of this. We didn't talk about our expectations: what Sarah's role would be, what the sessions would be like, how directive or not Sarah or I would be – and I was very unconfident about dealing with any of that. So we ended up with a very mixed idea of what was going to happen in these weekly half-hour sessions.

I had never worked with a child with those disabilities. There was so little she could do! She couldn't play anything independently, she wasn't using her voice at all, she would look at instruments to indicate what she wanted to play... for a long time we battled. We would offer Sinead the choice of instruments, she would show us which instrument she wanted to play, she would look, be very excited, be very clear as to which one she wanted, and we would go through this huge palaver of arranging instruments so she could play them.

Once we were all set up, I would be ready to play at the piano, we'd all be ready to start – and her mouth would go down. The one really strong communication she had was 'no'! Her mouth would turn down and that would be it. She was not going to play. And it was awful – it felt so mixed. She would come to the music therapy room every week, look really excited and be very clear about what she wanted to play, and then once it was there, she wouldn't play.

If Sarah tried to help her, support her arm, move her arm or her hands, Sinead would pull back and go into spasm, and then it was really hard to work with her. And look daggers at us. And where the difficulty came between myself and Sarah was in our way of thinking about what was going on, and of dealing with it. Sarah felt that this was about Sinead making a choice and communicating something, and if you've said you want to play this, then let's play it. My thinking was more about the feeling of it: how confusing that Sinead is saying, 'yes I want to play' and 'no I don't want to', and what is this all about. Sarah's concern was to get her to play, and mine was much more that it would be nice if she *did* play, but what is going on here… what's happening, in the room, now, between the three of us.

This child had such power… she drove me mad! She paralysed me – that's the word, paralysed! We were impotent.

This went on for two terms – there were little bits of playing: we had a 'hello' song, and a 'goodbye' song, and there were little bits in the middle and sometimes she would play. If we got the instruments sorted, her movements were so limited that Sarah would often end up making the movement for her – and then it would be basically Sarah and I improvising with Sinead's arm in the middle of it. That felt horrible and pointless… and what about Sinead? Where was she in that? She disappeared. She looked resigned: 'here's my arm, it's nothing to do with me – people are doing things to me and for me…'.

That was the quality of the early work. I didn't know what I was doing. I dreaded every week… and what was Sarah thinking about music therapy? That this was to help Sinead to communicate, giving her an alternative way of communicating, and Sinead did not want it …. There were also a lot of expectations from Molly in the class: how was Sinead doing, was she playing, singing… well… no, actually she sits there most of the time looking really cross, doing nothing.

In the end we decided that since Sinead wasn't needing help to play and she wasn't really playing in any case, Sarah would stop coming.

On reflection, it seems that we just got into this cycle of wanting Sinead to 'do' things. We wanted her to be a music therapy client, we wanted her to play, to sing – the idea of music therapy giving her another way of communicating seems so grandiose! It didn't take into account who she was, at that point! Music therapy emphasized so much that she *couldn't* do. She could choose something, but when it was there she couldn't play it. Her disabilities were being accentuated….

For me, the experience of sitting there with Sinead, week after week, feeling that I could do nothing... that I was supposed to be offering her something, and I had nothing to offer her that she wanted. I couldn't find a way to work with her, I couldn't do anything. I felt frustrated, limited and disabled... that was what it came to. It took me a while to get to that point. But that was really where I'd ended up: that this was what it was like to be her – people try to do things for you, to you, you feel that you can't do it, can't do anything, you feel paralysed! There it was! That was exactly the feeling, and this is the reality of her physical state.

Sinead: The duet

I was quite relieved to be on my own with Sinead. I was pregnant and was going to be going off for maternity leave at the end of that third term.

I had been having ongoing supervision, and in that third term I went back to what Sinead was doing. Here and now. We are trying to meet, we don't really need the instruments, we don't need another person, we just need Sinead and me. Whatever music comes out of that, we will do. I started just to play with her breathing. So simple really. If we were sitting in silence, then I would use the phrasing of her breathing. She understood straight away – she got it... *I* got it!!

Then everything happened very quickly. She started changing her breathing or holding her breath and then breathing again and enjoying the music going with her breathing .... she started to laugh... we both started to enjoy it, and started to make a game of it! And also I could reflect much more directly any movements that she did make – any little movements of her arm. If she was sitting next to me at the piano, if she put her hands on the keys but they didn't actually make a sound, then I worked with the movement as though she had made a sound – actually reflecting that back musically. She started to use her voice a little bit – it just came out of the breathing. She was starting little sighing sounds, and those got a little stronger, and we began to have a dialogue between us in the music. Which was simple at first: Sinead made a sound, then I, then her. This developed quite rapidly....

Her voice started to change. She started to find this really gutsy voice, whereas everything had been little breathy sounds. She found a much deeper voice… and began to make more distinct sounds like 'yes'.

That happened in the summer term. She knew I was going and we worked towards saying goodbye. I was going off to have a baby, and every week our sessions were more exciting….

> On the video clip, Sinead is small, frail, with a mop of reddish hair – her large alert face watches Claire closely. Sinead is strapped into her wheelchair to support her body, and she is on Claire's right, at the piano. Claire is tall, blond, and totally focused on Sinead: her body half-turned towards her, watching her closely. This does not seem too direct or imposing, but rather, it is the total commitment of one person to another.
>
> Claire sings a song that has developed out of their breathing and making sounds together: 'I can sing, listen to me sing'. Claire's piano playing is detached and light, with momentum in it as well as stillness. The music tapers off and presents a space, a silence which is part of the music. Sinead makes a sound within the space that Claire offers. The physical effort of her vocalizing is enormous. Her sounds are long sounds, on the long out breath, which Claire then colours with her rich, warm piano music and her singing. The music is lively and this fits – somehow – Sinead's inert form. Claire seems to make what Sinead does (and doesn't do) part of her singing, part of her own playing at the piano.

That's right! And also I *assume* an intention from her. I *expect* a communicative intention from her in what she is doing. So even when she is only moving her fingers lightly on the piano, I take that as her *actually* playing the piano, because that tiny movement is the most that she can do. I draw her into the music in that way, make her part of it as much as possible. I amplify some of what she does, I take little things and make meaning out of them, I make them part of the framework of the music. I expect a response from her! I wait at the end of phrases for her next movement or sound; I think about giving weight to what she can do – and I value her communications. I wait, I listen, I pare things down to the size of frame that she operates within…. Really trying to meet her where she is, without… all that earlier stuff about offering her instruments to play and getting her to play the way that I wanted her to! I was imposing my language, without waiting to find out hers….

Then I left to have my baby. It felt so hard to leave her and leave the work. We'd had an immense struggle, on all sorts of levels. For me as a music therapist, this was such a new area of work, and I'd had to really think about, to consider, how I worked with her. We'd found a point of meeting, we had taken off, gone a long way together, with her using her voice which she didn't do at other times. Her different voices: the soft voices, the gutsy voices. We were having lots of fun and she was enjoying the humour of being listened to, the anticipation, and having the kind of communication that is not possible for her verbally. And how her power had changed, from being a power of withdrawing to a power of engaging, to being an agent, to making something happen between us in the music!

Sinead worked with Rosie, another music therapist who did a locum for me for a whole year. I don't know very much about what they did, but they did start writing some songs together. Sinead was starting to use Rebus charts to communicate (with pictures on) and would often bring those into the sessions and show Rosie what she'd been doing at the weekend, people she'd seen, and they started to make songs together... some of the songs were wistful. That is what I know about their work: lots of improvisation, lots of vocalizing, not so much other instruments....

Sinead: Year two

I went back the following year, after having had Imogen, and worked with Sinead again for another year. She had seen me once during the year, when I had taken Imogen in as a baby. She understood that I'd gone to have a baby... though when I left she didn't know – I didn't know – whether I would be going back. During the last term of her work with Rosie they talked about their work ending and me coming back again.... I never found out very much about their work; it felt private, that was their year. No, we did not do songs together when I went back, that was their work, hers and Rosie's.

Sinead and I slipped easily into working together. It felt like picking up. Our first session back together, she was alert, excited, we did a lovely free improvisation and she contributed many sounds. The music had a strong sense of pulse, she was using her voice much more freely, there were whole vocal phrases. It was so very nice for me to see her again… her movements were stronger, she was using the piano a bit more.

Then the music began to change. As our work progressed in this second year, the humour receded. The work became much more harrowing. Everything got darker. I think that in the year with Rosie, when they were writing songs and starting to talk about people and feelings about people in her life, a different emotional understanding and language was beginning to grow from within Sinead… she was seven getting to eight. Then coming back to working with me, her emotional expressiveness in music became much stronger. We'd built good foundations in our first year together, despite all its difficulties, and had found a way of connecting musically. Now in the beginning of the second year of our work, she was going to use that. And the work had a very different feeling.

At this point, also, there was such a marked contrast between how she was in the classroom and what she was doing in music therapy. I would pick her up in the classroom, see her having fun, being very playful, and she was playful with me as I met her in the classroom. I'd wheel her down to the music therapy room, we'd get into the room, and it was like something being switched on…. Before I started doing anything, out would come this voice with these big tense movements – sometimes her body would contract, and out would spill these sounds … even if she'd had words, I would not have heard them, really… I would have heard their sounds. The feelings of her sounds.

She was so much more tense, and there was such a different look on her face when she was making these sounds… it was all so different to the quality of our earlier work, where she had been relaxed, making little, soft, playful sounds. This felt gut-wrenching: her contorted face, her huge mouth – I couldn't get anywhere near making the sounds that she was making. Her sounds were really raw, very powerful. The music needed to be powerful for and with her, it needed to be big. And I would sing about her having a big voice 'here I am with my big voice'. Because it was huge, her voice, it felt huge at the time….

On the whole, I think that our second year of working together allowed the darkness in her. It was like giving birth, allowing a fuller being... to the whole of this child, this person. The emotional texture of our work did not feel like that of a seven- or eight-year-old, and that quite worried me at one stage. I would think, was it just too much, what I was doing. I don't think it was. But if the seven- or eight-year-olds that I know were doing that, talking in that kind of way, or howling, it would feel dreadful... far more dreadful. But Sinead doesn't have the distractions that an ordinary seven-year-old has. She's got herself, and she thinks a lot.... And then, at the end of the session, it would be like switching again. I would often be in the classroom just a bit after the session and find her happy, smiling, smiling at everybody.... Whenever I saw her outside the music therapy room, in the school, there was hardly any connection; between us. We had a secret connection; she didn't need me out of the music therapy room... our connection happened in music therapy.

> In the second video clip, the harmonies of Claire's piano playing are strong, their colour dark, the chord clusters fuller. Claire plays continuously and sings strongly, and Sinead joins in with long strong phrases. She does not need to be given the space in order to 'respond', as in the previous clip. Her voice rises and falls; there is incredible tension in her body... her relationship with Claire, through music, has a tautness, and this tautness is reflected in the music, both hers and Claire's. Although Claire improvises the music, the music is part of them both: Sinead is as much part of the improvisation as is Claire. The music has a minor feel, the clusters reflect tensions... harmonic tension, even dissonance at times.

She gives me so many clues as to what to play and how: the feeling of being with her – her body, her posture. The question of how do I know what to play and am I inferring things about her...? No! I am not making any verbal interpretation of what she is feeling, or what she feels like. I feel her directly! I don't have time to think or to interpret: I *know* her feelings, her posture, her face and vocal sounds, their tension, her clenched fists – all of these inform my music, in the harmonies and rhythms that I use. So that she can experience her feelings through the music. She doesn't have to be alone with her feelings: and our work is not necessarily to *change* her feelings. I accept them, manage them (both in me and musically), and make it possible for them to be shared.

If we'd had our jolly 'hello' song and our very structured music – if I hadn't been able to feel that I could contain her darkness and pain, then it wouldn't have happened. We would have had lovely times, and probably worked much more on the developmental side of things and specific areas of communication: you know, we could have worked on developing her vocal sounds, her arm movements, and so on. But that wasn't how it went. I responded to her, to other aspects of her, to her emotional life. And she felt that. If she hadn't felt this, then she wouldn't have picked up on this different, darker, colour and texture so very quickly. She would have changed what she was doing, she would have stopped me doing it. She wouldn't have allowed this unless she felt safe in expressing her darkness and pain. You must remember that Sinead knew how to say 'no'!

When I talked with her class teacher about her (in fact she observed some of those sessions through a one way mirror), Molly felt that Sinead had an immense amount to deal with: not just with her disability, but her life in general.... Molly felt that this work in music therapy was so important for Sinead – there was nowhere else where Sinead could just be. Molly knew that she couldn't be like that in the classroom.

The humour was still there though – quite a bit.... For her birthday, a lot of the session was playing around with 'Happy Birthday', she was so excited about her birthday! We sang about who was going to be at her party, what she was having, and we improvised a song about her being eight – and next year I'll be nine, and last year I was seven – and she would put the sounds in with her voice....

I worked with Sinead through two pregnancies and two births. I was frightened of having a child with those disabilities.... When I went back to work with Sinead, it felt strange that my one-year-old could do more than she could do.... One of the strongest things that has come out of being a mother is allowing and managing the darkness, and putting this back into my music therapy work. All those feelings of having to manage the rage, the sadness, the darker bits, and to come out of them, to allow them, believe them... that had a big impact on me.... With Sinead a lot of my experience was about believing: believing what I was doing, what she was doing, and who she is... who we were, together in the sessions.

There was a feeling of equality in our work, of a mutual language in the way of being... an understanding of each other, operating at the same level, somehow, where the disability didn't matter.... Our work felt very intimate, until the session finished. From when the door opened, then it felt different. And then the disability was so much more apparent. It would hit me. Again.

Also, it felt so challenging to work with her vocalizing: it felt enormously stretching, emotionally. This was about meeting her musically, finding that voice in myself, the harmonies on the piano, the texture that is right – that is challenge enough, but it is more than that – it is the emotional, the feeling meeting as well... and that is really hard....

Working with Sinead I have felt really limited; I have felt musically very frustrated, that I cannot do what I want to do. If I wanted to, I could look at these limitations musically and find that there are things I could change in my music, and do differently, but this is not enough! That is looking only at the music and how the music can change without listening to its meaning and *feeling* its meaning... it is so important to *feel* limited and frustrated! That is part of being with Sinead, of being limited in what you want to do... of being unable to do it.

I think that for Sinead and children like her, there is a big investment in being happy, and other people have a big investment in them being happy, being smiley. When they cannot communicate very much else, they have to smile.... A lot of the time this has to do with the difficulties that people around them have in seeing them as they really might be.

Reflections

How to be a music therapy client

One of the reasons that the initial sessions with Sinead were so exasperating for Claire (and for Sinead) was that there were two therapists: Sarah, the speech therapist, and Claire, the music therapist. They had not had a chance to check out with each other what each of their roles was with Sinead; and how music therapy could address some of the issues in her life. This situation is not uncommon: even if Sarah and Claire *had* discussed the sessions beforehand, each might still have experienced the actual event, in the music therapy room, quite differently.

Sarah, as a speech therapist, is focused on speech and language, on the mechanisms of communication, on how best to help someone like Sinead make herself understood in the world, and how best to receive information from the world. These are crucial skills for Sinead with her limited capacity to make herself understood. As a speech therapist, Sarah hears the music that Claire plays as inviting Sinead to communicate with her, as developing and supporting whatever minute expression Sinead makes, and giving it communicative meaning.

But what happens? Sinead will not play. Her communication is strong: neither Claire nor Sinead misinterpret her 'no'. Sinead makes herself perfectly clear. At this point, the two therapists begin to part company, and all three are in trouble.

Claire feels dreadful: what are they doing with Sinead, apart from 'taking her arm'? Sarah undoubtedly feels lost, what on earth is Claire doing or not doing? And Sinead – well, Sinead is the focus of the session, but somehow she is not quite being the client that they both need her to be.

And then there is a beautiful turning point. Claire, with help from her ongoing supervision, has been reflecting on what it feels like to be Sinead. They breathe together – it is so simple! They share the beginning, the length, the end of a breath together. And the breath becomes a sound – at first Claire's sound. This is a precious moment of transformation. Sinead lets Claire know, very quickly, that they have found the key to their work together, the key to giving Sinead a sense of agency: Sinead *can* be part of creating the music *with* Claire, rather than having it done *for* her. From now on, their work unfolds quickly. And then Claire leaves to have her baby.

Creating darkness

In their second year of working together, music therapy becomes dark and painful for both Claire and Sinead. Claire experiences the work as harrowing; she feels Sinead's tense and dark feelings, and presents these to Sinead in her playing. Claire has no time to think, to interpret, to distance herself from these feelings. She feels them herself, they are distressing to her, and she puts these feelings into music. So that Sinead can hear her *own* feelings being known by another, being shared with another human being. So that Sinead can participate in the music of her feelings. The music that Claire plays is not only the music of Sinead's feelings: it is also the music of Claire responding to Sinead. The music is of their joint feelings; of the tensions in Sinead's posture and vocal sounds, of the contours of her emotional expression – as well as of Claire's own feelings in response to Sinead. Sinead is not alone in her tensions and frustrations – her feelings are known by, and shared with, Claire.

But why create darkness? Why not support Sinead's happy, smiling side, which obviously makes her popular and attracts people to her? Music therapy gives us an emotional vocabulary: we feel, colour and enhance our feelings, and we extend them, through music, through sound, through hearing and feeling ourselves in music, through *being* music. Sinead has a lot of feelings inside her: feelings of pain, of frustration. This is why she comes to music therapy in the first place. She has learnt that smiling is what makes her physical condition 'bearable' for us all. But Sinead is a complex child, far 'older' in a sense, than her seven years: she has time to reflect on her life, and to think about who she is. She also knows – and this may be an unconscious knowing – that because of the foundations in their first year together, Claire is willing to allow the dark difficult feelings that Sinead feels. Claire will not brush them aside; she will not insist on being only jolly together in music therapy: this would be an emotional/therapeutic restriction – or imposition – on Claire's part.

Without accessing our dark and terrible feelings, without giving them a voice, we remain incomplete human beings. We keep these feelings tucked away because we only know them as negative, frightening and ugly. We do not give ourselves the opportunity of feeling the darkness as having great beauty – its own kind of beauty – and enriching our lives. For Sinead, experiencing and sharing her pain and darkness directly in music therapy can be seen as a rite of passage towards becoming a more complete emotional person.

Claire is not afraid of darkness, of feeling it in herself and in others, and of managing rage. Her training as a music therapist, her clinical supervision, and having her own very young children, has given her a direct, inner knowing – not just a theoretical or textbook knowing – that even dark and dreadful feelings need to be felt, acknowledged and managed. And Sinead is ready for this – Sinead knows very clearly how to say 'no', and were she not ready to give voice to her dark feelings together with Claire, then she would have forced Claire to continue playing light happy music. And Claire would have done just that. As music therapists, we cannot insist on anyone feeling what they are not ready to feel, or on them being part of music that they do not experience as being related to them. At the same time, though, as music therapists we have a responsibility not to avoid darkness and pain, perhaps because of our own discomfort with it. This is one of the reasons that clinical supervision is critical: Claire is accompanied on her journey with Sinead; she is helped to see what feelings she might be avoiding, what feelings in Sinead she may be missing – and why this might be. And, as we see in this tale, darkness does not invalidate the humour and fun that is just as much part of their relationship. Indeed, darkness makes their relationship richer, more complete.

CHAPTER 4

Giorgos
Isolation in a Hospital Ward[1]

The setting

Nicky is at the keyboard in a hospital ward. Next to her is a small person with a large head, composed and intensely present in the moment. He resembles an old man – almost a Buddha figure – and uses his hands in a declamatory style as he sings. He sings with his entire body, with enormous pressure from his chest. There is no ambivalence about his presence in the music with Nicky. Every now and then he scratches his large, bald, blind head, takes a deep breath and enters into an expansive, sustained vocalization, accompanied by Nicky at the keyboard. As he sings, his hands move in a beautiful flow, drawing the music in the air, the music flooding out of him, into him.... Nicky's spontaneous playing at the piano opens the music for him, and he expands into it, like an opera singer, interweaving with her playing. This old old voice, in this old old soul. All of four years old. About to die.

The children I work with have life-threatening illnesses – they are not necessarily terminally ill. Some are born with an immune problem, while others come in suddenly diagnosed. They often come to the hospital as a last resort. Some parts of the acute ward are raw places, where people – families – have just been told the news, and I witness

---

1   Based on the interview with Nicky O'Neill. Nicky works at Greenwich Healthcare, specializing in early intervention, autism and assessment, at a children's hospital, and at the Nordoff-Robbins Music Therapy Centre in London.

53

them taking it all in and dealing with this. I let them settle for a few days, and get used to the environment.

The hospital environment is structured around disease: its effects on the children, how they respond to it, and on the curing procedures. Both children and parents become preoccupied with blood counts, temperature charts – the disease is very powerful. It is difficult to maintain any normality, and difficult for the children to have any sense of worth other than having this powerful event happening inside them. So often they do just give in, hence their passivity and under-stimulation. They lose control or lose interest in structure and predictability; they lose their sense of time – that is how chaotic and timeless day and night become, because the disease does what it will, has its own time. The disease rules, and the killing of it rules as well. The hospital is chaotic – time and space depend on the disease – and this makes setting up music therapy sessions so difficult. We all – staff members too – have little control over our day. Autonomy is lost: as soon as the pattern and power of the disease is known, then children and parents give over autonomy to the medical environment.

I am there one day a week, and the children get to know that when they see me it is a Wednesday. I have a trolley which I wheel around the wards. I am present, visible, available and familiar, so that the child or parent can ask for my services at any time of the day. I think that this is vital, and the deepest music therapy relationships have started from the basis of a child saying, 'I want to play those...'. I do not always wait for referrals and I don't have referral forms. There is no time for all that, and everyone should have access to music therapy. And in any case, creativity is at the bottom of the treatment pile: how will creativity help to kill disease?

I have to use instruments that are wipeable, because of sterility, and I cannot use blown instruments. This is a great shame as babies, especially, often lose their voice when they come in, usually the result of traumatic shock. They just glaze, and blown instruments would be so useful but this is not possible. I also have a large, very good keyboard, a variety of drums, and lots of small instrument for the babies. I have as much variety of sound as possible, and the sound quality of my instruments is excellent. Sound is what the children become robbed of. In a hospital setting, and especially in the sealed wards, their aural sense becomes limited, often listening to machines clicking and clunking all day and night. The children can become visually preoccupied, staring at a video or computer screen all day long. The older ones in particular, become computer obsessed. Computers help them to 'switch off' and remove them from the horrendous situation that they are in. Many of the children tend to become very visually based and passive, partly the result of feeling unwell and, if you think about it, what else is there to do for all those hours each day?

Giorgos

Giorgos was born in Cyprus, with osteopetrosis, a disease which results in a thickening of the bones, especially in the skull. This results in pressure over the cortical nerve, which, in his case, is damaged. He is visually impaired, and although the disease can be arrested, it cannot be cured – the damage is irreversible. The next stage, if the disease were not arrested, could be for him to lose his hearing. He is not very mobile, and his legs are weak: in fact he is one of those visually impaired people who is very careful, who is not able to revel in his body. He is very static, and spends the day sitting on his chair upright in his hospital room, or lying on the bed. He is small for a four-year-old, with a very distended stomach, skinny little legs that are bowed due to lack of use and deformity. He has bulbous eyes because of his visual impairment, and a very, very large bald head. He is a Greek-Cypriot child of normal intelligence, speaks no English, and has come to Britain with his parents for treatment.

He has a tape recorder in his hospital room and tapes everything: conversations, someone walking into his room, hospital noises, whatever there is to tape. He plays the recording back to himself and laughs at the top of his voice, commenting on it in Greek and laughing raucously. He has created this aural world which he can control, fuelling his imagination… but at the same time, this world accentuates his isolation. This is the only conversation that he can hold, and maybe he has done it out of his need to stimulate himself. Otherwise his verbal and emotional interactions, at the level at which he is able to function, are only with his parents.

He was referred to music therapy by the ward, as they knew prior to admission that he was responsive to music and had special needs that they couldn't meet. I went into his room to meet him, with my trolley. He sat next to me at the keyboard and played bits here and there – I call it 'fluttering'. Our musical contact was minimal: he would hang on to the edge of the keyboard and do bits of sounds here and there – and then chatter away in Greek, laughing. He seemed to enjoy the sessions – and asked his mum whether he could do this every day. Initially the sessions were difficult for me, and quite disconcerting. When he did his fluttering I would try to imitate a sound or pick up a rhythm, but he was like a butterfly just landing and then off again, he was so quick! And unpredictable! His rhythm constantly changed, his chattering was fast, his speaking was Greek.... I didn't have any words to hang on to, which in some ways was good, it really made me listen to his sounds, to his voice. The mood of the music was very intense, at times almost hysterical: he laughed a lot, he shouted, the veins would stand out on his temples. Fleetingly I was able to catch the odd note out of his chatter... he would sometimes land on a note and I could sing it, or I could hear that his voice was occasionally influenced by what I was playing or singing. Most of what I was doing was to try and reflect his mood in my music, to reflect my experience of him. Whenever I managed to catch a tone or a mood, he would move off. Our contact was minimal, and frustrating for me. It was almost a defensive chatter, he would not let me into his world, he would not let me share his sounds, he kept me out. I didn't know what to make of him. He wouldn't play any of the other instruments at first. I had the interpreter in for the first session, to see if we could communicate in a basic way – for instance, tell me if he was in pain or needed to go to the toilet or finish, so she taught him those words. Because I wanted it to be safe in there. His mother would sit outside during our sessions, so it was just him and me.

The sessions with him lasted between forty and forty-five minutes. In my experience, the sessions with the children in the hospital are much longer than with non-hospitalized children, and very, very intense. The children are very focused: I don't know whether they are thirsty for that amount and level of contact. In music therapy, they are in control of the contact, the session, the space… the relationship, the music.

Then he went into isolation – medical isolation. In some ways it didn't seem to affect him as much as it does other children because he was so static, and had so little contact with the outside world anyway. I was asked to work with him in the isolation ward, which I mostly don't go into because of restrictions on the number of people who visit there – but nobody could communicate with him so directly. I had to wear an apron, make sure my instruments were well wiped… but my dirty shoes did not seem to matter!

His bone marrow transplant happened during his time in medical isolation. The child's marrow is eradicated and a new one is donated. The new one hangs in a bag above their bed while they watch TV, eat, sleep… the image that I have is of the child's living self being replaced by someone else. They give over part of their livingness… and that can often cause problems for some children who might be receiving marrow from a forty-year-old woman, for instance, or they might be taking in something of the opposite sex…. I don't know how much was explained to him, how much he understood or whether he knew what was happening to him.

In the medical isolation ward children cannot see other children unless they walk past. They usually hear adults talking about so-and-so, and how they are doing, how the disease, the cure is doing, but there is no direct peer contact unless by 'phone. Any contact is very disease focused… the pressure and whole focus is on the drugs and dealing with the disease as soon and as effectively as possible. Quality of life is talked about – but isn't really present. It is all about drugs and blood counts and statistics…. Moreover, adult relationships are supposed to protect you as child and make sense of the world, but the parent can't do that any longer. Here, the child may be hurt in front of them and they can't protect the child – so the children's sense of relationship becomes distorted. I suppose that my relationship with the children in the hospital is probably the only one that is not treatment centred. I don't come in because of a treatment need – I do not enter into the frame of illness-treatment, and choose not to see myself as just ministering to the part of the person that has a disease. I see my role rather as counteracting the effects of disease and treatment – or not even that: as playing/working with the child.

Anyway, he was in medical isolation, having his transplant, and in the second week there was a change in our music – this was our fourth session. He was chattering away as usual, sitting next to me at the keyboard, and then the speed of our music started slowing. I became more insistent musically about focusing on the notes that he was offering, and the speed came down even more. Maybe I was stronger, more confident, more assertive, more insistent: I held on for a longer time, I didn't let him just flutter here and there as he had been doing. The whole quality of his voice began to change. It was as though he was becoming a fifty, a sixty-year-old man! There was a totally different level of interaction between us. The music became much more intimate: I was supporting him with my playing, he was totally influenced by what I was doing... he was influencing me, we were creating music together.

It was extremely intense musically – a bit like East meets West: him, this Greek Cypriot four-year-old, with no way of speaking to me, an English-speaking adult... and yet through our music-making we connected totally. I couldn't get my voice to match his quality, and in fact I stopped trying. I find it astonishing that even when you cannot match somebody's vocal quality, and you don't have to, you still remain connected as two separate individuals. Occasionally I would sing too – almost a Bach-like sequence of notes repeated, coming down, which somehow fitted to what he was doing. We were together. He had lost a lot of his vocal tone during this time in isolation – he'd had a very ringing tone to his voice before this. His voice had become almost more breath-like, although there were definite tones to it. But this was like from another planet – extraordinary singing! Hardly the singing from a four-year-old! Almost like that of a religious singer, his voice had a lot of oscillations... I could imagine him singing in a holy place.

I felt that he was singing about himself – about a self that neither he nor I nor anybody on the ward had experienced before.... It had a meditative quality, that you get from somebody who is in another place, or centred, I don't know what it is.... The nature of his existence, perhaps his illness, had led him to be a much deeper, older person because he had so much time thinking, so much time being on his own. I know that he used to sing on his own as well, but I don't know if he sang with that sort of quality.

He was in and out of transplant reasonably quickly: six weeks. And then he had a nasty experience, and became more ill. A painful skin biopsy didn't stop bleeding for a long time. Following this, he stopped using his voice – both in the music therapy sessions and outside sessions. He became withdrawn, he didn't appear to be able to play with the assurance that I had experienced in him before. He lost confidence in relating to me so he was quite held back; our music making wasn't very definite, but he did want to try, and tried different instruments. Our music became quite different at this time. Whereas it had become so free, unpredictable, energetic, intimate... the music we now made together became very structured, predictable, boring. It was not our music at all!! I found it difficult to concentrate, and I think that he found it difficult to be present. It was almost as though we were making music for the sake of it. The music was very childish, in major keys – I was trying different sorts of keys, offerings, and began to try different instruments – he would try one of the other instruments and then another. We were trying instead of doing.

If we think about structure once more, whether in the day, in the hospital, structure in music... children need consistency, something to depend on, something that is predictable. In hospital, the only thing that can be depended on is that they will get their drugs at a certain fixed time. Apart from this, they are in a very warped way of life – everything has changed, and continues to do so. The children become so acclimatized to it, so quickly, although the parents mostly do not acclimatize to this in the same way. I feel that the fact that children adapt so quickly to this chaotic, disease-controlled environment doesn't mean that it is right. It could be seen as a defence mechanism and will affect them in later life. If they get to later life. So I see myself as trying to provide some normality: a trusting adult relationship; structure, routine, the things we take for granted in our lives outside. What happens to the child and their sense of confidence, their spontaneity – they can become quite frightened of being spontaneous, hence the passivity. It is easier to switch off.

This is what I think happened with Giorgos. He was beginning to live – to express, to relate in such a free and wonderful way – with me, another person, rather than being in his own isolated individual world. And remember that he was blind… so that the trauma of this event must have been amplified. And it is not surprising that the free, spontaneous, extremely rich music regressed, if you like: we *had* to become childish, helpless. We needed musical structure – almost like nursery rhymes – nearer to a four-year-old's music, I suppose, at this time of deep personal uncertainty and mistrust of the world around him.

We had one more session after this traumatic time. He became well after the transplant and was able to go and stay with an aunt, although he was still in and out of hospital. Somehow he just could not keep well enough to return to Cyprus. We didn't know it was going to be our last session, and he was much better. He was the most well he had been since before the trauma. I could hear that his voice had returned, and he had regained some of his confidence. We did some free singing together, his voice was triumphant….

And then one night he died. About three weeks later. One of his parents' last requests was for a copy of the video of his last session. I am not in contact with them at the moment. They have returned to Cyprus.

Coda

What I am doing is giving the children at the hospital an experience: one that you sometimes cannot qualify, justify, except to say that it should be allowed to happen. It is very difficult for me to verbally explain what we are doing in the sessions, for example, in a psycho-social ward meeting. How *can* I explain this musical, non-verbal, highly intimate experience? The mere experience is apparently not sufficient – it has to be framed, explained… and so I video sessions, and when they see these tapes, professionals are touched, and they do understand… but it is not exactly part of the medical model.

I am creating the space, holding on to it and believing in it… and, you know, it can be very difficult to stop people coming into the room and interrupting the music therapy session. When I first worked there a doctor came in and said, can you just keep playing while I examine this child…. I don't let *that* happen any more.

I played the video of the work with Giorgos to the staff on the ward. They saw him singing his heart out – they'd never seen him like that! And of course not, because music therapy is such a rare setting within the acute ward especially; a setting so private, when everything is so very public. Music creates a space for the child, to reach that level of emotion and interaction. It transforms the arid, sterile, clean hospital environment that allows no mess – into being quite disturbing and alive, powerful, private, intense and so very rich. It is difficult to set up this special space, and so difficult to preserve – but on the other hand people may not want that sort of space – it is also painful.

What this work has done to me is to change my perspective on the world. Before I went there, I thought there was a reason for everything – you could work out why things were supposed to happen, look on the positive or whatever side of every situation. But what I have encountered on the wards is just tragic. I hadn't understood the meaning of tragedy before – children facing situations that encompass pain, removal from life, and often just a horrible way to die, because often they have horrendous lives, the last few months… It has put into perspective the rest of my life, and made me understand the immediate – another word I hadn't understood before. If I don't see a child there and then, when they are well enough, they could well be dead by next week, and I don't have time for filling in forms and waiting to find out if there is a good-enough reason for them to have music therapy.

The power of music… it is extraordinary: it gives back life! A child will be quite definitely invigorated after a session – and me too. It is a relief to get into the room where we will make music together, create an island of life and colour… create intimacy. But it is so difficult to hang on to, in that setting. The setting erodes intimacy, does not want it that much. If the children were on that ward to die, my role would be much more valued. But they are there to be 'cured' – rather than kept alive… often they are not… cured or kept alive.

Reflections

Here is a child who lives in 'another world'. He doesn't 'understand' too much since he speaks Greek, and the hospital environment is a buzzing, booming mass of 'alien' sounds: machines, hospital noises, and English human sounds that do not make sense. Inventive and lively child that he is, he 'plays' with the sounds of his environment, recording them, playing them back to himself. He derives great pleasure from, in some small way at least, being able to control this rather unmanageable and overwhelming environment.

Here comes Nicky with her musical instruments, and no, she is not 'treating' his 'disease'. So why is she there? She is there to play. Play? When you are dying of illness? Are these music therapists crazy? Yes.

Let's think about playing. When we play, as children, we pretend certain things, we replay aspects of life, and try them out in different ways. So we might try teddy sitting over here after a day's work, his feet up, reading the paper and smoking a pipe, and he is cross with dolly because she is sick and has not cooked supper, and she simply will not get better… and now dolly is in bed covered with a blanket and teddy says 'I'd better call the doctor to be quick quick quick'…. the doctor came with his cane and his hat, and he knocked on the door with a rat-a-tat-tat.' [2] And so on. There are no wrong or right ways of playing – playing unfolds as we go along. Unless, of course, there is a game with certain rules, but as we know, children are endlessly flexible in negotiating and re-negotiating the rules of games amongst themselves.

Let's think about playing in music therapy. Giorgos' playing on the keyboard is a 'fluttering' here and there like a butterfly. This is him, these are the sounds that give him pleasure, that present him to Nicky, as they both play on the keyboard. She cannot 'catch' him: musically he is all over the place. For her this is frustrating, for him, it might be a great game of 'catch-me-if-you-can'. Where else in life can this ill child dodge and run and skip and not be 'caught'?

In hospital, the contours, surprises and smells of life are at a standstill. In hospital there is no weather, no gusts of wind or rain, no

2   English Nursery Rhyme: *Miss Polly had a Dolly.*

deep, dark night or day. There are machines that clunk and chunk steadily, unvaried smells of medicine and sterile environments, colours that do not change, and temperatures that are controlled. In music, Giorgos can be free to create the sounds he wants to, to make as much noise as he wants, to become another kind of rhythm. He can live freely, imaginatively, he does not need to be 'ill', he does not need to be 'dying'.

Music offers him another structure, another dimension; a pliable one that he can share with another person, intimately. Giorgos has little intimacy in the hospital: no-one speaks his home language apart from his parents and the interpreter. And there is another kind of isolation – what we might think of as a spiritual/emotional loneliness. Music therapy reveals his remarkable knowing of 'other' aspects of living, and the intimacy between Nicky and himself is more than a musical one.

This intimacy is also painful. Not so much the pain of illness or of life ending. Rather, it is the pain of being enlivened and quickened when we glimpse another way of being. The pain of growing and expanding towards who we fully are – and the losses that this growing incurs. Giorgos unfurls towards his extraordinary singing, towards this ancient age – perhaps he is leaving behind his childhood. Nicky experiences him as an old soul. This is something to do with the intensity of his long, melodic phrases, the quality of his voice, the dignity and clarity of his arm movements as he sings, and the music that is steady, slower than his usual fluttering. It is as though he allows her, he *needs* her to be with him during this special kindling of the spirit. She feels an intense affinity with an essential part of Giorgos. It is his core humanity: this is beyond a four-year-old, and let's even forget that soon he will die. At the very core of our being is a timeless essence that we all recognize when we allow it. At this centre of being, Giorgos may well be a four-year-old *and* an old person.

Nicky cannot explain the feeling of his singing, and indeed, if we think only in clinical or psychological terms, then it is difficult to understand. She talks of East meeting West, of a religious or holy quality, of a meditative experience, certainly a transcendent one. As Nicky and Giorgos enter their 'sacred' music, long flowing melodies begin to emerge; phrases of exquisite contour, of emotional focus and intensity. These are reminiscent of the melismatic chants of sacred liturgies – of Hildegaard of Bingen, of the Latin, Greek Orthodox and Gregorian Masses, and of the Jewish liturgical chants. Nicky calls the music 'holy'.... and this does not seem far-fetched or sentimental, but essential and mysterious.

What happens musically, in these moments?

The first thing Nicky says, is that their music slows down. Not his music, or her music, but *theirs* – this is a shared event. His fluttering begins to be 'held' by her playing. This may be because she is more insistent, more determined to focus him musically – and it may be that only now, in their fourth session, he is ready to be anchored and 'held' by the music. And this 'holding', incidentally, in no way dismisses or diminishes his fluttering. *That* is also part of him.

Nicky's 'hunch' is that there is more to him than his musical fluttering. Her hunch is not just intuition – it is what we might call *clinically informed* intuition: Nicky is an experienced music therapist, and the many other children with whom she has worked have left imprints on her work and her intuition. These imprints now contribute to her work with Giorgos, just as their work together will enrich her work with other children after him.

Nicky cannot quite match Giorgos' voice quality – and here we remind ourselves of the distinction between meeting the notes themselves – which as a musician, she can do – and meeting the *texture* of his voice. This she cannot reproduce. East meets West, she says – as though Giorgos can remain who he is, within his own culture, with utmost certainty and authenticity – while Nicky remains who she is: she does not try to become Greek-Cypriot in order to meet him. Their commitment to their shared music ensures that their differences are consonant, and complementary. Their alliance has an intimacy which is more than just 'parallel' playing, with each happening to coincide with the other occasionally. Here is close-knit cooperation – so close-knit, that they do not need to be doing the same thing at the same time. Each needs the other, and depends on the other – in the healthiest and most creative sense – for this awesome, timeless, intimate music. With a four-year-old.

PART II

Music Therapy with Adults

CHAPTER 5

Martha
Working with Wellness[1]

Music and life: Ebbings and flowings

I grew up in Cork, Ireland, with a lot of music, a lot of singing, I played the piano, everybody sang. At weddings, at home doing the washing up, driving the car, it was all singing, and you had a song that was associated with you. When you got together at a party you sang your song: it was a song that people would expect to hear you sing before you sang something else, and if you sang something else first, they would say 'oh no, what about – you sing that other one, don't you, what is it now…?' And I enjoyed all of that: listening to people singing their song, the kind of slight arguments about when they didn't sing their song, the talk afterwards… you sing it because you like it and then if you are heard singing it, you are expected to sing it again the next time. When you sing it, it becomes your song – I don't know why – the song finds you a little bit. At one stage I had a song which I wasn't totally happy with being my song. It was called Bantry Bay and I'd still be asked to sing it all the time, I didn't think it suited my voice – it was very high – and there was something about the lyrics that I wasn't completely happy with either. I remember one rather romantic and idyllic view of women, 'and the fisher girl with baskets swinging…'. It was also a lovely song, and for a while it was the song I was asked to sing. I'd be dying to move

1 Based on the interview with Catherine O'Leary. Catherine lives in Nottingham, where she has a private practice, and is a Fellow of the Association of Music and Imagery (AMI).

on to another song. I think your song can change at different stages of your life – it is nothing very definite – not at all. That whole experience of singing of songs, the songs in your life, is very much part of the way I think about music and the work I do now as a music therapist.

I don't know exactly where the urge to do music therapy came from, but it was there before I went to university in Cork, and my studies were always focused in that direction. I trained as a music therapist at the Guildhall School of Music in London in 1977, after University. I studied with Juliette Alvin and enjoyed her enormously. We had some strong battles! Then I worked in the East End of London for a year, hauling instruments around sixteen day centres each week... after a year, Juliette arranged for me to work in the US. This was one of the times in my life that I felt I was in the right place doing what I wanted to do at the right time.... I worked outside Philadelphia in a large psychiatric hospital , with a forensic unit, a drug and alcohol abuse unit, quite well known, a teenage unit and long-stay and acute wards. I worked on nearly every department. There were four senior music therapists, and I was regarded as one of those, and four interning music therapists. The department was fantastic: we had a whole floor of the building, one area had a bay window and two grand pianos, every instrument of the orchestra was there. There was a room for rock band instruments, electric pianos... there were several practice rooms with pianos in them, listening rooms, and a record library. It was the time that I felt, here I am, I have everything at my disposal, now what can I do.... I found it wonderful, extraordinary. And the music that flowed out of me! That was something I had not experienced, even playing, performing – the music was just flowing all the time, so freely, effortlessly, beautifully!

I returned from there to Ireland and it was exactly the opposite: nobody had heard of music therapy. I got a part-time job in the psychiatric hospital, did some work with autistic children in their homes, and also in a special school. But there were no instruments, it was a struggle.... I was the only music therapist in the country. There was a lot of interest in music therapy as people got to know about it, but it was unsupported in every practical way – not enough money for instruments, no proper place allocated. And yet music was a real and dynamic part of people's lives! Music was as alive in the hospital where I worked as it had been in my own family! These experiences, as well as later experiences when we moved to England, fulfilled my expectations of how difficult working in an institution can be....

As my own life was changing, I began thinking about moving towards another area of music therapy.... I felt more and more that there are a lot of people who are well and who could benefit from having music therapy.... I was having children, meeting a lot of women who were having children, people who were taking time out, time to reflect. At times like these we are often faced with questions on the meaningfulness of our lives: where are we going, what is it all about? I was at this point in my life. Then someone who came to my home said, 'have you heard of Guided Imagery in Music?' (GIM) and I realized that I had, but had forgotten all about it. She told me somebody was coming to Britain, so I immediately checked in and that was it – that was my way into working with people who are well. They may be in crisis, but are out there and working in the world. And development begins at the point of wellness. I started therapy myself, Jungian therapy.

Guided Imagery in Music

It was Helen Bonny who, in the late 1960s in the United States, began to develop a specific music therapy method called GIM. It is now officially known as the Bonny Method of Guided Imagery and Music. She'd been involved as a music therapist in pioneering work with Dr Walter Pahnke, Stanislov Grof, Hans Karl Leuner and Joan Kellogg – these are all famous names now – and they looked at the effects of hallucinogenic drugs on consciousness and on altered states. Helen Bonny realized that working with music *without* the drugs was even more effective in gaining insight, and you didn't have to worry about the side effects of the drugs. In GIM, clients image while they are in a relaxed state.

As we work now in GIM sessions, there are four sections: a period of time spent talking, moving into relaxation time. The relaxed state is very important, moving from normal consciousness into a relaxed state which facilitates the flow of imagery. As the client, you recline, your feet up, covered with a nice blanket and I relax you either with a visual imagery relaxation, a physical relaxation or whatever suits you. Then you move into the listening to the music, and this is when the imaging takes place. The imaging is induced by the music. The music is mainly classical, and it is chosen as for any music therapy session, to match how you are that day: your mood, feeling state, energy level, and where you are in the therapy. We choose from a range of especially selected, mainly Western classical music. This is because it has been shown that people seem to access the widest range of imagery with classical music… Helen Bonny found that when people chose folk music or popular music from their past, the imagery was more limited to memory and association. There is ongoing research into imaging with different kinds of music, but the selection that Helen Bonny chose works very well indeed.

As you listen to the music, you begin to image and you speak out the imagery. The imagery is not directed by me, as the therapist, but I am there so that you are not lost in this world. I might respond with 'hmmm, aha…', and I might ask things like 'can you tell me a bit more about that, how does that feel, what else do you see?' The point of asking questions is to intensify the experience for the traveller – that is the client, and the therapist is known as the guide. I work together with the music: the music and the guide are co-workers. I am in tune with both you and the music, listening to where you are going, to where the music is going – and staying very much in tune with what is happening, while at the same time writing the transcript of what you are saying. The music facilitates the process: it is a container, a companion, it is dynamic, it moves, it is allowing the experience. We are all used to transformation and transpersonal states in our relationship with music – even if we have never thought about it – and conscious imagery is very much part of our musical nature.

People come in and out of the image. The music will evoke an image, then they get totally caught up in that image and are unaware of the music. Sometimes people come out of the imagery world completely and then they go back into the music. It is not as simple as the imagery fitting the music: it can be like that but everyone images differently.

At the end of the music listening period, which is usually for thirty to forty minutes, it is time for you to come back, so there is a period of adjusting back, sitting up, and then a period of talking again. This has a dual role. The talking brings you back to a normal state of consciousness, so that you are ready to walk out the door, and it allows the imagery to begin to resonate for you. It is not a time where we take the session apart... because the images are easily reduced to a small part of what they can mean. There is a danger of fixing on one idea and missing a lot of what else has happened. So we review the session, note what images are standing out in particular for you, and encourage you to think about the imagery over the next week, or until the next session. I may invite you to do a mandala as another means of helping to access the self. I would offer you a sheet of paper on which a circle of about ten or eleven inches in diameter is outlined. The idea is to focus on the circle and when you feel ready, choose a colour that attracts you and allow yourself to draw. There are no rules. The circle is an archetypal symbol of wholeness and the mandala that is drawn can be understood as a reflection of the self. In GIM the therapeutic work with mandalas has its roots in the work of Jung and that of Joan Kellogg, an American art therapist who has specialized in working with mandalas for the past twenty years or so. The idea is to allow the imagery to begin to resonate in your life, and for you to get to know these inner spaces rather than adapting these spaces to your habitual ways of thinking. You take away a copy of the transcript.

The main focus of the work with clients is on the content of the images. Nothing in an image is unnecessary, and there is nothing that is without meaning. I am fascinated by things like right and left – people say there is a stream on my right and a field on my left, it could never be the other way round to them... it just doesn't *happen* to be on the right... or on the left. Every single thing is significant. Anybody can image sitting in a field, but the texture, the colours, the surroundings, the feelings, are entirely different for each person. Every single thing about the image contains information. The image is like a cross-section of what is going on for that person.

We image in different ways. We have images that are based on reality, on memory, mythical images, spiritual images and kinaesthetic ones. I don't know if there is a hierarchy of images – I think rather that there is a mixture of images from different dimensions of our lives, that merge into one another. They merge in a way that would never happen consciously. For example, parents or relatives who have died and who come back into the present situation: into what looks like your home setting right now, which, of course, they would never have known while they were alive. Or experiencing yourself as a bird somewhere. Time and space and reality and myth combine in images to give us quite a different – and much richer – experience of our lives.

One woman I worked with had suffered from sexual abuse and she had an image that was very important to her, of a very large beautiful black woman. This woman was stunningly beautiful and became her mentor, her guide. In one of her imagings, she was looking at a man, or a man wanted to dance with her, and she didn't even want to look at him. This guide took him and turned him around and she was able to see him: in her imaging, her guide showed him to her, that was her role in the imagery. Another time, the guide appeared to her, and it was as if she could call on her for advice at almost any other time in her life... and the description of her sounded extraordinary: she was large, beautiful and black... and it sounded like a very important figure for her.... Of course, in her conscious, biographical life, she hadn't a clue where this guide came from! So you see, you cannot think about these things deterministically!

The image is usually a moving image rather than static, because the music is moving – you are moving through the image and experiencing it while you listen. That is very much easier than if you were imaging without music: you could get stuck at any point... but in GIM the music changes and moves on and the imagery does too... it is extraordinary really. I feel incredibly privileged to be in that space with someone.

Martha

A middle-aged lady came recently, she was very, very upset. She'd had two people in her life become severely angry with her out of the blue, phoning her up and being abusive. At the same time she was moving house which was extremely tiring.

While Martha talked I listened to how she was, to how she was walking, standing, sitting, talking, feeling, being. Sometimes I could hear music, I could almost hear what piece she was 'playing'... I could hear a whole resonance, a complexity of sounds... I tried once to write this music down but the notes we have were not appropriate to the sounds I was hearing. I listened also to what piece of music I heard playing in my ear – that was to be the piece of music that I would choose for the imaging. At the same time I was listening to what music we were sounding together, while she spoke and I listened and responded to her. I was listening in musical terms.

For each person that comes to see me I am aware that I listen to only the current section of their music or their resonance... for Martha, there was also music that came before this piece here in the session, and music that would play after this time in her life. As Martha spoke to me, I was at this particular point of the music of her life. And I was thinking, 'what is the music that came before this, what has led up to this? And what is the music that will sound after this?' That music is impossible to write down, but I allow it to resonate for me.

I was interested in the *actual* music of her life as well. In a way, the one is a reflection of the other. You see, the music that people like, that they are drawn to, and the music that they choose to play and sing and be involved in, reflects that other music, the music that is the music of their life.... In Cork, when I grew up, my song was totally part of who I was, for a period of my life. As I grew and changed, I needed to change songs. This is at the external, biographical level – there are other levels of existence, and these have their own music. As music therapists, we talk about clients' rhythm, their timing, the timbre of their voice, their own sounds, the pitch... almost their biological music, if you like, and the music of their feeling states. But there is also the music of their soul: of their journey through life, and the timing and rhythm and sound of that. So when somebody comes to me, I am aware of all of this – I am listening to this movement at this time, the music here in the room, that is part of us both, and I am very aware of all the other music that has gone before that – and also their own music, to do with other levels of their lives.

So with Martha, as she talked and I listened, I felt her tiredness and what I was hearing in the immediate was about her anger, and also that she had begun to move on within herself, through her own processing. She reclined, put her feet up, she was covered with a blanket, and began to move from normal consciousness towards a relaxed state. At this stage I didn't need to draw her attention to her exhaustion. I took her attention from her body and directed it towards a focusing image which had come out of her talking: people sometimes show you, in their talking, what they want or need to focus on. Or else you can offer an image – something like a place in nature – from which they can begin to image.

For Martha, I chose Brahms' Symphony No 3, the *allegro con brio*. As she listened to the music and looked closely at the image that had come to her, she realized she was in a little village in Cornwall. She was talking over the music, she may not even have been aware that she was hearing the music as the image engrossed her more. For Martha, the music evoked this village in Cornwall. She explained afterwards that she had gone to this village as a young girl at a time when there was enormous tension in her family, a lot of it directed at her. This little village had been a paradise for her; it was the most restful place she'd ever been in her life. Now, her psyche had chosen to start the session at this place – she had no idea when she was lying down relaxing that this would happen, but this is where she found herself. And this is an extraordinary thing, that there is a part of us that does this: it was both acknowledging the difficult time that she'd had now as an adult, by drawing a parallel with when she was little, and yet, at the same time, it was placing her there, a place of healing and nurture, preparing her to go on from there.

This happens over and over again in GIM: there is a level of knowing that we already have which is surprising to us – even though we are doing it ourselves, it is part of our psyche – and the more we trust it and get in touch with it, the more we settle down in our lives.

Martha also had another image, in a different session. This time, we were listening to Samuel Barber's *Adagio for Strings*, and the image was that she came through a black world with sharp black rocks and thorny bushes tearing at her skin. There were images of war, death and destruction all around in that world, such a difficult journey. The music changed to Gounod's 'St Cecilia Mass', the *Offertoire* and the *Sanctus*, and she ended up on a bridge, a suspension bridge, not very stable, over a huge gorge. Way way below was the river. Ahead of her lay even worse pain… not attractive at all, so she couldn't go back, or forward, and down below was too far, there was no way down… and she felt completely stuck. Now, my experience of GIM is that you do not remain stuck. The psyche finds a way through – but what that will be… is rarely predictable. As a guide I have to trust that also, and not step in to rescue. She said, 'now I'm really cross and I spin around'. And there on the other side of the bridge, the river was a small brook running so close to the bridge that she could dip her aching hand in it. The brook was gentle and there was a boat there! Her answer was to turn around on the spot! It was enormously empowering for Martha! But what exactly was going on there? The answer wasn't in the future, and it wasn't in the past: it was taking another look at the present…. There is another perspective to this: it was looking in another direction of the present. And, you see, if we take another look at where we are – and it is not something we can do in our head, it is not something we can work out – but if we allow ourselves to stay still rather than move 'forward' all the time, just keep still, relax with it… and just be there… we may get another perspective. And interestingly enough, a lot of spiritual and mystical traditions are about getting into the moment, rather than out of it – being present in the moment. The answer is there where you are… but we all tend to spend our time looking forward to see where the answer is.

Levels of meaning

GIM is not a problem-solving technique, it is an uncovering one. It is a way of listening to ourselves. The more people get to know the inner self the more they relax. I find that often people come to therapy very tense seeing life right there and then in terms of the problem which is upfront: it is the first – and sometimes the only – thing they see and know. It can be a very narrow context. GIM allows you to look at difficulties from different perspectives in the imagery. The context is widened by this experience and the wider context is part of *you*, more of you than you usually allow into play into your life. The greater space allows for understanding to take place and the wider context helps to make things meaningful. Another thing that happens is that the deeper we go into ourselves, the more whole and complex we are and at the same time, the more we are part of the whole. We are part of a world where duality is left behind and where everything is one.

I believe that all time is present in the present moment. We live and die by a linear system of time, and our bodies age by that. At this level, our present seems governed by our past… so Martha's response to the difficulties in her life as an adult may well have been governed by her experience of the anger directed towards her as a young child. But there are other patterns in our lives, 'deeper' levels, where our lives aren't simply governed by the past. At these levels our present is as much a part of our future as of our past, only we can't see it. I think of it as similar to music: each note in a piece of music stands alone, but we also hear it in relation to the notes that went before and – when we know a piece – we also hear that note in relation to what follows. It has a meaning within the context of the piece as a whole and is part of the feeling of the piece as a whole.

As I continue to work with someone, I begin to see emerging in the flow of imagery, a rhythm and timing, tension and resolution, places of rest and places of great activity. I see this as the emerging wholeness of their life. I have in the past made graphs of this flow, and it's like another image!

What I am talking about here is not the content, like the content of the problem that is causing the tension, but the tension *itself*. And when people relax or the problem is resolved, what I'm interested in when I draw it out, is not what helped with that problem, but the fact that they are feeling less tension. By doing this I get the feeling for their own music, their own resonances – at different levels of their life. This is not part of GIM generally, it is my own way of hearing things.

For me music and images are very compatible, they both allows us to access different states of consciousness, and to experience a transformation of the present moment, to see more in the here and now.

By and large, in the West, we live pressurized and materialistic lives and yet there is more music around than ever. Recently I was struck by the imagery of a typical record shop. Have you noticed how you come in from the immediate reality, the sounds of the road, and usually the first thing you hear are the sounds of the day, the pop music section..., then you go further into the store and you might begin to hear jazz, folk, soul music..., and then even further still, furthest from the outside, usually behind glass doors or even on a different level, you meet the quietest, deepest level... classical music... you often have to search it out at the back of the store, coming from the immediate through to the timeless, the longer lasting... this is an image in itself!

Maybe we need music as a balance to the pressures. I think we are so fortunate to be living at a time when we are expanding our boundaries to include more levels of consciousness and transpersonal material. And today, something as solid as science is exploring and making these other levels and dimensions of our lives accessible. And of course, music is also at the heart of this. In music therapy we are constantly working with other levels of consciousness and ways of knowing. Our whole inability to talk about our work is partly because we haven't got the language to describe what these dimensions are – yet. But we will have.

Reflections

Images exist within us in our psyches, ready to be evoked and known by us, ready to be experienced, to add meaning, texture and colour to our lives. However, our images can remain unknown, unnecessary, somewhere within – or out there. We are more than able to live our lives 'on the surface' without images: do the 'right' things, accumulate a good 'biography'... until Martha's 'crisis' brings her to music therapy. And evokes images that enable her to transform 'crisis' towards broader understandings of herself.

This story differs from others in this book, because Martha does not play or improvise music with Catherine. Together they *listen* to music. Before listening to music, while Martha talks, Catherine listens to her talking, and to something else as well: to another kind of music, the 'music' of this person – the music of her life, her soul, of her journey through life.

What are we to make of this 'other' music?

Catherine understands and experiences life in terms of various levels and dimensions of music, sounds and resonances. Some of these dimensions are internal and intangible: they cannot be conventionally notated into music as we generally think of it (and perhaps, to try and 'capture' these in some way would limit their impulses). Other dimensions of music we know well: the external, biographical music of our culture, our ancestry and our social group. Catherine alludes to music as embracing a rich, complex diversity. There is music that is 'musical' and that we experience externally: neurologically, physically, aesthetically and culturally. There is music that we might call 'emotional', i.e., the timing, intensity, shape and patterns of our feelings: the swoosh, the bursts, the slow light trickles, what the philosopher Suzanne Langer calls the 'morphology of feeling'. These can be portrayed in music, whether improvised or pre-composed, and we hear, recognize and resonate with these 'musical' contours of feelings and emotions. There is also music that we might call 'psychological': the rhythm, timing, intensity of our expressive and communicative gestures, movements, the prosody of our speech, and the flexibility and adapting of these as we communicate with, and receive communication from, another person. Then there is music that is 'spiritual': the music of public/cultural and of private spirituality. The religious works of Palestrina, Bach, Schubert, John Taverner, and Arvo Pärt – are part of formal and public religious tradition and culture; while the music of private prayer or meditation includes ancient mantras that protect us from negativity and evoke an atmosphere of personal sacredness. There is also the 'music of the cosmos', or the music of the spheres, which we may not know consciously, or hear in our 'outer' lives.

All of these – and no doubt other – dimensions are part of the music of our lives: music as art form, as social/cultural experience, as meditation, music as therapy. The great Sufi musician, Inayat Khan, talks of music as a sacred art: he says that the music that we play and hear (the external music) is a part of the music of the whole universe, it is part of everything, part of the oneness of being. Here, music – like life – has no beginning, middle or end, and is present in this moment. Catherine is aware of, and listens to, all of these musics, all of these times – past, present and future – as Martha talks: the biographical music which has a present, past and future, and the universal music that *is* – eternally. Now.

As in music, so, it seems, in life. The 'biographical' or linear level of living does not resonate alone. There are other deeply mysterious knowings, both personal and collective, that impact on our lives. The beautiful exotic black woman who enters the imagings of the client is available to be a guide when needed: she comes from another level and another time of knowing and wisdom. Where or how remains a mystery – and mystery needs respect, rather than 'solving' at a biographical or linear level of life. Catherine and the client allow the mystery and work with the image. In doing so, they include various dimensions of life in the present, in the same way that the music that Catherine hears, and works with, is not only about art form, emotions, or psychological acts.

Catherine's task is complex. She needs to ensure that her listening to Martha is acute, needs to provide music that will enable Martha to unfold towards her own images *and* enable the images to begin to resonate for and with Martha. She carries and accompanies Martha through the painful, and at times daunting process of uncovering the meaning of her images – and invites Martha not to 'close' the meaning of the image too soon. Too quick an interpretation of an image can result in a 'false' certainty, one that our intellect finds comfortable and comforting – leaving our imagination deprived of full and complex meanings. In GIM, clients 'hold' images in mind until the next session, allowing them to resonate in all the dimensions of their lives.

The psyche's capacity to create images is the locus of GIM work. These images may emerge from other levels of our existence, and as such, do not easily 'make sense'. This is especially so when they are viewed through the cold lens of 'neon-lit' reason – the reason that is the legacy of the age of Enlightenment. But there are other kinds of reason, other rigours of thought and reflection: and here, Catherine's role is to make as much sense as possible of these images, with Martha. This 'sense' needs to be as complex as is Martha's reality. Thus, the image of finding herself on a bridge may have a multitude of meanings and understandings, which take time to show themselves. And this multiplicity of meaning is what Catherine, through her training and her listening skills, enables, together with Martha.

CHAPTER 6

Mary and Steve
Creativity and Terminal Illness[1]

Prologues

Improvisation in Music therapy

The biggest impact of the music therapy training was learning to improvise. This was a totally new way of experiencing myself in music. It wasn't just experiencing improvisation or learning it, or finding that I could do it. It was having a new experience of myself in music. Because even though I'd had this long relationship with music, doing a lot of performing and travelling around, I didn't really relate to it, I felt somehow separate from it. As a performer, playing all this music that I learned, it was something there on the outside and I played the notes. This didn't move me, it didn't really come from within me. Also, this new experience of improvising music was very much linked to being part of the group of music therapy students, and experiencing myself *and* the group through music improvisation.

In learning to improvise, the music begins from inside me, and I had this feeling of it being lifted out, I was lifted with it, I came out of myself with it, it drew me out of myself. What happened in the improvisation groups was intensely intimate: it was about experiencing myself, as well as being experienced by others, in music. The improvisations were like a merging of different things – of being separate and yet part of... of

1   Based on the interview with Nigel Hartley. Nigel works at the Nordoff-Robbins Music Therapy Centre in London and at Sir Michael Sobell House in Oxford.

being intimate but not personal… the paradoxes that are there in music therapy all the time….

Institutions and theories

I'd already had a training in counselling, based on Carl Rogers' person-centred approach, and also took in psychodynamic theories. I found that this didn't easily fit with music therapy and this was a surprise, because for me it would have been the most natural thing to do, to take psychodynamic theory into music therapy! After all, psychodynamic theories explain relationships between people, surely they should help to explain relationships in music. For a while I tried to make these theories fit into music therapy, and couldn't….

I feel strongly that our work is influenced by the institutions that we work in. Although I didn't realize it at the time, working in a children's institution that was heavily based on the medical model, there was this pressure to work 'psychodynamically'. This was an enormous struggle for me: something didn't fit. I would be trying to work out what the music was about for this child… so that I could go to the inter-disciplinary staff meeting and talk intelligently…. But a lot of the time I didn't know what was happening! I was using psychodynamic 'speak' as a way of pretending that I knew what was happening, yet I didn't feel that what I was saying was what was happening at all! The words weren't coming from inside of me – just as in the past when I performed and the music didn't come from the inside….

So I felt this enormous struggle, thinking that I can't do this work, there is part of the jigsaw missing. I wanted to have a deeper understanding of what I was doing, and tried using psychodynamic concepts – these just didn't seem right for music therapy. I think that it was also a very personal thing: I was battling, throughout this time, with my own relationship to music.

Not long before I left this institution, I made a decision: I wasn't going to babble on any more. At a case conference, attended by psychiatrists, nurses, psychologists and social workers, I played a tape of the session and said, 'I've no idea what is going on in the session, here is the music – can we talk about it'. Colleagues found it so fascinating to eventually hear some 'live' music therapy! I think it helped them to realize that what is happening in the music is different to what we *say* and *think* is happening. I'd always felt in meetings before, that there'd been some kind of tolerance of music therapy. I suspect that people thought that music therapy was trying to do what they did. So, for example, the psychiatrist would think I was trying to do what he did because I used his language, or the psychologist would think, 'he's just playing around with what I do'. But in listening to the tape, they understood how difficult it is to talk about the work – to put it into any coherent form. They could hear that music therapy was not doing what they did, and that it was vital to the life of the patient!

I think that we are very influenced by the institution we work in, and you get to a point where you think either you fit in with this philosophy and work in this way or get out. And maybe subconsciously I made a decision to get out. For me it wasn't the way that I was going....

Dying and creating

I like to think that I would respond in a certain way if I knew I was going to die – but we don't know until we are actually there, until something happens. Three years ago, after Steve died, I had an awful car crash that changed my life. My car turned over on the motorway, and I was unconscious.... At that very moment I knew I wasn't going to die, that this wasn't it. Here I am, working in a hospice with people who have all this time to die, and yet you can go bang, like that, with no preparation. The accident made me realize that however it happens, it is going to happen to all of us, and whatever we go through, whether it is quick, whether it is long, whether we know it, whether we don't, it is inevitable. There are lots of different ways death happens....

To me death is part of living – and sometimes with death there is an enormous ego thing, of letting go the importance of oneself within the world and realizing the smallness of who we are; the minuteness, in comparison to what it is that we belong to. And here, it is not dying that worries people, it is what is going to happen on the way there, the suffering, the pain, it is the *living* part of it. I can't help but feel anxious about that in relation to my own death, how will it happen, will I go through enormous suffering… the other thing is that we are alive to suffer. All of us suffer, and we carry it around with us and we go into it from time to time. It is a huge part of life, and we try and be in control of it. We are not in control at all.

Here at Sir Michael Sobell House, people come to music therapy not because they want to change, or want me to change them. They want to be with me, with another person, to experience being with someone, to be intimate. They don't come to music therapy because there is something 'wrong' with them. People come and experience themselves as being musicians, artists, as creating and being creative – at a time in their lives when it would seem unthinkable to be so. There is a quickness about our work together, because you get to the heart of the matter much more quickly. Our society sees death as a time of giving up, of deterioration, letting go, and here they are, dying *and* being creative and having new experiences of themselves that would have seemed impossible, unthinkable! It is a paradox of working with people who are dying.

For example, an elderly woman, Mary, asked could she see me. She had been in hospice for only a few days and was very quiet and timid. I brought her over in her wheelchair. She was completely wrapped in blankets all round her head. She was shaking. I talked a bit about music with her and she didn't say very much, I asked her could I put the tape recorder on, which I did. Off the blankets all came, and she said, 'I want to write a song… and the song is going to be called "why do I worry"… could you play a chord on the piano please'. So I did and off she went, making it up as she went along. Afterwards she listened back to the tape and said she wanted to change this and that, so we changed it all, and within an hour we'd written this song, and that was it. She was enormously worried about dying; her death was imminent. What she released in the song was some kind of affirmation that it didn't matter whether you worried or not, it was going to happen because it is part of being alive. I thought that her song was going to be incredibly moving, very sad, but it was quite happy in the end… she was saying things like 'I am not worried about dying because my husband loves me and he's going to be there and I'm going to see him again….' Her husband had died two years earlier. She needed to say this, say it in a complete way, and I was not going to interrupt her. I was not going to focus on what she was saying even though it was vitally important, I was going to provide a space for it to be said, held and put together.

She never came again. She didn't know what music therapy was, what it could be, but she knew what she wanted from me… it was this sense of time: it is now, and if I don't do it now I am not going to do it…. This event released something: music helped her make a complete, uninterrupted and affirmative statement at the end of her life… and even after that one session nurses on the ward were noticing how much more outgoing she was: she was asking for things, talking to people, there was some kind of relaxing, letting go. This allowed her to *live* – instead of dying for her remaining weeks.

What is interesting is the different length of time that I spend with people before they die. With one person I might work once a week for two years, and with another I might work for one session only. What I experience quite clearly is the same direction or level of being with them and journeying with them, even though the time scale might be so different. Within minutes of playing with someone we can go from this place to that, whereas with another person we do the same journeying over thirty sessions. Clients at the Lighthouse[2] would come, play, and go. They might have had no idea of what music therapy was, they might never have played music before, but they would come and know what they wanted from it in a very deep way. There's no messing around, no time for it, we'd go straight into playing, that's what they were there for. So instead of delving into what the music meant, what it was about, I simply stayed with the music and trusted it.

I realize more and more that the uniqueness of the therapist–patient relationship in music therapy is that we *play with* patients… we don't expect them to play alone – and for me this is the strength of the work.

2   The London Lighthouse offers care, support and empowerment to people affected by HIV and AIDS.

Steve (i)

Steve was my first adult client, my first ever 'dying' client. Our work together lasted two years. He was HIV positive. I was absolutely terrified: he'd had music therapy before so he'd have some expectations … and I didn't know whether I could be the music therapist he wanted me to be. I didn't know what to say when he first came, how to be with him, what do I do here, should I be in some kind of pseudo counselling mode? As soon as we started playing together, I felt a huge relief, like this was where we should be, this is it. That was my first experience of really feeling 'I am a music therapist!' – after two years of working with learning-disabled children and adults, and also with children and adolescents in psychiatry.

Enormous music started to happen with Steve, and I started thinking that this was because he'd had music therapy before. He would come, we would improvise together for an hour and he would go, and there would be no reflection on it. He was not interested in reflecting, so I was left alone with this enormous music. I then asked myself what this music was about for him, why was it important for Steve to have an experience of himself in music.

Of course he would let his feelings out, that was part of it, but then, he could have done that alone. No, I think there was something about my involvement in the music *with* him… this is why it was so important: for him to have this experience of himself in music – with me. My responsibility was to be as open, flexible, and as accepting of him as possible when we played music. So the question became, 'what kind of musician does Steve need me to be in order for him to experience himself in music?' As a music therapist, I have this enormous wealth of musical experience and have this responsibility to provide, depending on the person's needs, and what they are asking from me.

It was in my work with Steve that I began to understand that this was my task: to be in music with clients and to give them the experience of themselves in music.

He taught me a lot about the work. He demanded such a wide range of musical styles and responses: he would come and drum, and his drumming was like nothing I had every experienced in my life… I don't like using the word chaotic, but there was nothing repeated! He drummed all the time, with no space for me to be heard, and every time I tried to catch or to meet what he was playing, he would take off somewhere else! His playing was more like a collection of noises and sounds than anything cohesive or what we would think of as being music. He was completely hard work! Then, out of the blue, he'd let me hang on to something in the music with him, and there would be no rhyme or reason why he would do it at that point... our pulse would coincide, or my harmonies would 'fit' his drumming... but this was fleeting. Over two years, that drumming never changed: it never became more cohesive, more pulsed, more in the metre. Within it, though, were bits that he gradually allowed me to share with him. He would alter his playing and we would move towards each other... it was almost like flying through the air with someone, suddenly we would land... on this planet, experience music together and then go off again, land on another one – and none of these planets would be the same, musically. And yet it was just so intimate... the meeting was beyond anything I had ever experienced before... it was exhilarating.

Then I began to realize that he was making a conscious decision to play the drums like that. The drumming was not necessarily reflecting his inner life. What happened was that in one session after a few months of working with him, I was playing with him and getting really frustrated: I couldn't meet him musically, couldn't reach him, we seemed to be in different worlds except for those fleeting meetings! In this session, I was trying all kinds of things in the music to get him to play a pulse, be with me in that, and allow something to happen... and he'd been hitting the marimba with a drumstick, it was really percussive. There was no sense of melody at all, he was using it as another drum. I got so frustrated that I stood up, picked up a stick and whacked the marimba, straight across what he was doing.... He stopped playing and looked at me. He was really angry. He said 'is that a therapeutic technique?' I dug around in my mind for my best therapeutic technique and said 'well, are you upset because I invaded your space...?' He said, 'no, I'm upset because what you did had nothing to do with what I was playing'. I thought, what does he mean... and it turns out that he was a freak listener, he would go home and listen to people like Eddie Prévost, a group called AMM – a group of improvisers who would create a wash of sound together... and he just loved it and he was trying to recreate this music. He was making decisions of what he wanted, and he wasn't being what *I* wanted him to be....

As soon as I realized that I had gotten myself totally stuck on what I wanted him to be, I don't know whether what we actually *did* changed, but certainly my perception changed. Our playing became music as opposed to just noise... and although the 'landings-on-planets' music didn't change, the times in-between felt a lot more significant as opposed to thinking, 'oh god, we are just going through this in order to get there'. The bits in-between began to feel important. We both let go and were able to just be in the music – as opposed to trying to make it into something else – therapeutic improvisation, maybe! I was with him a lot more than I had been, in his trying to recreate something... which was what he wanted.

The most moving thing about working with him was that he died very quickly and unexpectedly. He had got ill a couple of times... and I got to thinking he's never going to die because he's been ill so many times. We had our last session on the Monday evening and he died the following Sunday morning... and I didn't know, I was expecting to see him the next week, and what had happened was that the virus very quickly got into his brain and he deteriorated rapidly. It was a dreadful shock.

Suffering and structure

I cannot remain separate from suffering – mental, physical, emotional. I hear it, and I certainly feel it, in music. Sometimes, suffering is unbearable for people. Sometimes it is unbearable for me to be there, with them in their suffering. But once we begin to play together, we have a context to put the suffering in. In music, suffering can be made more bearable, it can be put into the space, it can be heard and moulded and formed into something that is concrete. And beautiful. Art and music can come out of enormous suffering. So when you and the person are meeting in that suffering in music, it becomes more bearable. I don't mean that I take on this other person's suffering for them, but my own suffering is there as well. I cannot keep that apart, it is impossible in music to remain distant from that – there is this merging together. This person realizes that it is as much me as them, and we are creating this way of being, this way of holding something together.

The whole question of structure in music is so important. Music has boundaries, it can hold. The structure in music is sometimes the only structure that we have. For example, seeing someone at a certain time every week is almost impossible here: if people are not feeling too good, they are anxious to see the doctor and there is no point in them seeing me before they see the doctor. Other boundaries and structures that we usually put into place in therapy seem to be stripped away. We are left with what we do. It doesn't matter where we do it, or when – but rather that we do it, that we make music. Music has its own boundaries, it can contain, hold, shape, make things safe in a way. Music is where the meeting, the suffering, the intimacy happens. Sometimes everything else is stripped away, and there is only music to hold what we have got.

I do carry things around with me, things to do with suffering, fears, people's pain – and yes, I have the capacity for carrying – as have a lot of staff here at hospice. I understand carrying as having a space within myself that is there to take in experiences that I have with patients. It is carrying around things... pain, people's suffering, sadness, different forms of energy which we can then interpret or identify as feelings. In the making of music, I make use of that space all the time, and sometimes the space gets full up and I need to empty it. At other times it empties itself. Sometimes there is enormous joy, a lot of humour in a place like this, and also at the Lighthouse. There is never a feeling that you cannot mention death – it is there all the time... death becomes part of life and part of life is laughing and being humorous. People ask me regularly, 'how do you cope with being around so much death?' Well – I've had some of my most intense experiences of being alive in my work at hospice!

I do have a priest that I go and see – not that I am an enormously religious person, but there are things that come up in this work that I feel more comfortable talking to him about than I perhaps would to a therapist. And I cycle – and I love the feeling at the end of the day of getting on my bike and cycling just nowhere in particular... travelling and not knowing where I am going is a release… and not to know how I got there or why I'm there and turn around and come back. It helps me shed the things that I carry.

Steve (ii)

When people die, they don't just live in our memory, they live in us. It is something to do with eternity; people just carry on living in the people they have touched deeply when they were alive. Steve has been very important to me. With him I really learned my craft, I learned what I could do, what I could do well, and I let go of wanting him to be who I needed him to be and just let him be who he was…. I do miss him, and every time I listen to the work, our work together, there is this incredibly moving work, the final session.

In our final session – we didn't know it was going to be the final one – there was a lot of drumming, it was busy, rhythmic, and it got to the last two minutes and we swapped over, with him playing the piano and me the drums. Suddenly the whole thing changes. It is as though, in the music, a stillness opens…. I hear it in his touch on the piano… this is the end of two years of enormous work with someone…. I want to play you the recording of the last one-and-a-half minutes….

> You can hear Steve's touch change at the piano… at the beginning, the excerpt is very busy and full of sound, and then suddenly Steve plays three notes only. Nigel is on the drums, and fades to almost nothing. Only three notes repeated, with held pedal, both insistent and strong, and open at the same time… the rhythm expands, slightly and then more, Steve brings in bass notes of the piano, very deep and strong, open music… and then a long, held note, alone… and silence.

There is something almost infinite about it, the repetition, the simplicity, it is just so unlike him… and the fact that I could just disappear, be there very quietly underneath his playing. At the time, I didn't register that it was different. I hadn't remembered the session. When I listened back to the tape, I could hear that there was something significant, even though part of me thought, well am I just looking for something because I need an end to this work. But when I listen to it I feel quite accepting of what happened, of his dying so suddenly.

I felt angry that he had died, actually, that we hadn't finished the work. It felt more that we were in the middle of it. And yet there it is, in the music, that is the end, and I had no memory of it. On some deep level we probably both knew, and yet I had just blanked it off... because it just wasn't the right time for me to realize it.

Coda

Spirituality is a big part of this work, but there is no reason why it should not be part of all the work that we do. It is what we are working with.... A lot of people surprise themselves in music therapy. They come and think 'I can't play music', they do an improvisation and then can't believe it was them... and people also say that for them being in music is very similar to meditating. This makes complete sense. Meditation and prayer are about being in this space, however we access it. Spaces are there in life to be accessed, and there are different ways of getting into them... the experience of being in music, people describe as being the same space as prayer and meditation. People here at hospice talk about relating to something outside of themselves in music; they talk about the experience of being at one which can lift you outside of yourself....

Music is one of the greatest mysteries ever. It is like God, whatever God you believe in, or what you think of the world – an enormous mystery that can never be solved, however much we delve around and try and understand. We will never be able to understand and put it into a box, and neither should we. We have this need to understand everything, and if we can give something a label, then we think it is safe. I think we should avoid this.

I was very sceptical about Paul Nordoff, even during the training and also in my years of working. Over the last year, though, I have listened to a lot of his work and the man was a genius! His whole way of being! I watched again the video of him in 'Parents and Children', and I hadn't watched it for ages. In the video he says a lot of the things that I find myself saying. He says that with a child, whether they headbang or whatever they do, we take what the child brings and we give it back to them in music, and they have a new experience of themselves, and that is it! That is what we do all the time, this is the strength of working in this way.

And I find that inspiring really, that he is saying that, because it is where I feel I am coming to… and my ongoing supervision has also inspired me enormously. I did the training course and never really took in what the work was all about, and somehow only now am I beginning to find this, through the work and the people I have worked with. Now, in listening to Paul Nordoff's work, it is such an inspiration! And at times I am quite shocked by it, because it can be quite crude, and at times it is incredibly quick and very direct. I find it enlivening, this man knew what he was doing.…

Also, talking to people who knew him at the end of his life, there was an urgency in him: he had something to do, something to pass on to people. Because he knew he was dying. He had cancer. And the years that he was here in London, running that first training course, in the early 1970s, he knew that he didn't have any time, he had to do it now.

This rings true for the work I am doing.

Reflections

Being in music

The people who have music therapy with Nigel are not coming in order to be 'cured' of their terminal conditions, or even to 'change'. They are people who are well – and who are more aware of their death than most of us are of ours. They come to music therapy and experience themselves *as musicians*, as creative people having new experiences of themselves in the last stretch of their lives.

Here we touch on the creativity that is inherent in us all, regardless of whether we are musicians, artists, unrhythmical or colour-blind. Mary needs to sing her song – to create her song – to form and give voice to all sorts of feelings and intuitions about her impending death. She may have only the vaguest notion of wanting to express something. During the process of improvising this song – in her only session – her thoughts 'pop out', almost in their final form, save for a few adjustments here and there. This weak, trembling woman who breathes with the help of oxygen, finds tremendous energy in order to express, create and experience something crucial and essential about the ending of her life.

The act of expressing is a powerful transforming experience. It is the power of this transformation that draws out of us all phenomenal energy…. For it is not simply us who play music, but we are ourselves played by it: music transforms us all. This has nothing to do with how 'musical' we are – but rather, with how responsive, flexible and susceptible we are to other human beings, and to life.

Through music, our suffering can becomes deeply beautiful, powerful and moving, accompanied and shared by the music therapist. Suffering ceases to be a lonely, eroding, bleak event. The stories of Mary and Steve capture the healing inherent *in the act* of creating, even if this healing is somewhat intangible, difficult to put into words, something that has another kind of rigour and logic – a non-verbal, musical one. The crux of expressing oneself – of becoming oneself – in music therapy is that it does not happen in a void. Mary could have done her song alone, in her room, and Steve could have bashed his drums in a soundproof garage. This expressing happens within a relationship with the music therapist. Nigel is more than just accompanying and supporting Mary: what he does at the piano is influenced by what she sings, and this in turn influences her, influences how she will sing the next bit of her song. Nigel allows himself to be susceptible and responsive to her, and it is this musical *and* personal vulnerability that enables them to meet intimately, instantly through music. There is a subtle interweaving of feeling between them that Nigel, because of his training and skill, can portray in his piano-playing. His playing is woven into her singing – and she 'knows' this.

The music that Nigel makes with Steve sounds chaotic, noisy, unbeautiful, almost manic. This is Steve's music, although, at first it is not quite his 'authentic' music: he is emulating music that he likes and feels strongly attracted to (and this suggests that there is something of him within this busy atonal improvisation). Nigel begins to sense that he and Steve are not quite together. Nigel is more than able, musically, to connect with Steve's drumming, and indeed, describes it as exhilarating. And yet, something is not quite right. They are not connecting *personally*. Steve is not being the client that Nigel 'needs' him to be – and here, we need to remember that Steve is Nigel's first adult self-referred client, and Nigel is vulnerable to this situation. After the incident with the marimba playing, where Steve angrily says that Nigel's playing 'has nothing to do with' what he, Steve, is doing, something shifts. With this comment, Steve reveals that he is aware of the personal relationship; he is aware that Nigel's playing is, at that moment, not relating to what he, Steve, is playing – and this angers him. Nigel's perception changes. Even though Steve's chaotic noisy drumming does not change, Nigel now hears it more fully: its meaning is richer, and they begin to connect personally.

What is the shift? What makes the difference? One difference for Nigel is 'letting go' – allowing himself to be in the music together with Steve rather than 'trying' to make it into 'therapeutic improvisation' or give it other theoretical meaning that Nigel finds unhelpful to his work. Here we return to the healing that is in the act of creativity itself: the very act is a healing one. And here, the healing is part of a chaotic and noisy event – one that Nigel, because of his insight and clinical skill, is able to hear *and to experience* as music. The difficult part of being a music therapist is that we are in the music *with the person*. We are available to whatever music the person brings, to however they play. At times, that music is deeply disturbing to us, personally and musically. And we cannot always 'turn back' and say 'oh no I don't want to play *that*'. Our commitment to the healing process is that we enter into the patient's suffering, pain, horror and beauty. And to the musical expression of this.

Carrying and holding

Music has boundaries: a melody goes this far, then it can be repeated, it can be followed by a different bit, then appear again and we recognize it. A melody can be played in different rhythms, it can be coloured by various harmonies, a successions of chords that give it different colours and textures. For example, the end of most popular tunes in Western culture is almost always what musicians call a perfect cadence. Most people 'know' this – whether they understand it as a perfect cadence or not. A cadential convention such as this one can 'hold' the players in music therapy improvisation. For example, the 'closing' or 'ending' implications of the perfect cadence can be in the therapist's mind during the improvisation with the client, even if the therapist does not *actually* play the cadence. In fact, Steve's musical renderings are probably contrary to the many traditional 'rules' of music. But the 'rules' give the therapist the option of moving or shifting the improvisation in a certain direction if necessary. Musical 'rules' can provide a boundary, a container for the improvisation, explicitly or implicitly – whether we use or discard them.

As the improvisation develops – and remember that improvisation is a spontaneous creating of sounds by *both* therapist and client – Nigel can hear its structure emerging: what bits fit together, whether these can be repeated or not, where another bit can be made longer, can be made bigger or tightened up, depending on what Steve is doing. He keeps these various bits in mind as he continues to meet Steve's playing. There may come a time when Nigel needs to 'pull together' the various 'threads' of their music. This may be because the playing is getting too dispersed for comfort (his or Steve's), or because Nigel feels that they might need to reconnect more strongly. Through his piano playing, Nigel can re-create one of the musical bits (a theme) that they have played before – he will do this within the context of their joint playing (rather than stopping and saying to Steve, 'lets do that bit again, shall we'). The chances are that Steve will recognize this 'theme', and will begin to move towards it in his drumming, bringing Nigel and Steve closer together in the music, as they 're-visit' familiar territory.

The significance of this is a therapeutic, interpersonal one: Nigel and Steve could go on and on and on, flying from one musical planet to the next – at some stage, though, a clinically-informed move by Nigel (and this happens extremely quickly and intuitively) may suggest that the improvisation needs to be drawn in, or folded within a structure that they have already created together. It is one of Nigel's tasks to remember what music they have played together, to bear in mind which bits might be useful, and to be able to reproduce these at some later stage, if necessary. While at the same time continuing to imbibe and create new music with Steve. A tremendously complex and demanding task. And an exhilarating one.

CHAPTER 7

Shireen
Into the Void of Brain Injury[1]

Prologue

As a cellist, when you play *basso continuo*, like in a Bach Mass, then you are supporting the entire fabric of the work. It is important to be extremely rhythmic when you move the bass note, as this creates a shift in the harmony, and the feeling of the music is also shifted. I love that experience of supporting and underpinning the music with someone singing *recitative* at the top. In many ways this links with being a music therapist: musically supporting the person in clinical improvisation, which results in shifting feelings and allowing or creating important moments. It is not so easy to put this into words, although the experience feels fundamental. And actually, the lowest note in a harmonic series is called the fundament! So for me it is often important to be *under* the music, supporting it....

Since becoming a music therapist, my cello playing has become so much more expressive: I listen better, I am a more accepting listener.... I hear music in more sounds... for example, I hear much more music in speech, and I also don't filter out or ignore noise as much as I used to. I used to intellectualize music and focus on the structure first, I used to be concerned about the individual notes rather than the overall flow.... At university as an undergraduate, I would be excited by complexity and big musical scores. I was drawn to conducting and would feel the power

1 Based on the interview with Cathy Durham. Cathy works in Bristol, in the community and with people who have learning disabilities.

of many instrument playing together. Now I'm much more interested in small things, few sounds, timing, real simplicity. In music therapy sessions, clients can express the most extraordinary individuality in their music, whether they are conscious of this or not. People may need to be heard in different ways. They tell you, really, how they want to be listened to… and maybe that is what I continue to develop as a music therapist: the capacity to listen in many different ways.

And I am much more at the mercy of music, it is more powerful for me now. I listen to music less than I used to; somehow I am more vulnerable to it. And silence is really important too. I give myself more opportunities for silence in everyday life.

Shireen

There is a woman I worked with for two and a half years in a neurological hospital in London. I will call her Shireen. She had a severe brain haemorrhage while she was seven months pregnant – she had very high blood pressure and this extreme hypertension caused a cerebral haematoma, a bleeding in her brain. The baby was delivered normally, while Shireen was in a coma. What a start to life! How could Shireen hold the baby, communicate with him the way a mother does?… She was in coma for about four weeks after her haematoma: it is very rare for anyone to be in a full coma for more than six weeks. She was in what we would call a 'waking' coma – she was showing sleep–wake cycle patterns, but was so unresponsive that her level of consciousness was unclear. I started seeing her about six months after her haemorrhage, to assess her for music therapy. Her brain was so severely damaged that there was no indication that she could make any purposeful movement at all. Shireen was in her thirties. She had two other young children.

Shireen was in a wheelchair and was fed through her stomach by a gastrostomy tube. She also had a tracheotomy to help her breathe… she had become blind… she moved her head from side to side, which indicated that she might be trying to pick up sounds. She could occasionally move her right hand to grab things, sometimes she tried to pull the tubes out. Often she would hold something but then didn't seem to know what to do with it. She rarely did anything functional with her hands. And her left foot would come off her footplate and stretch out… and go down again. This was something she did quite a lot, with no particular reason. The occupational therapists felt that it was a random movement, and not purposeful – all indications pointed to that. She didn't use her foot to respond to anything new that happened outside her body – if someone came up and spoke to her. I wondered whether her foot movement could be a response to emotions within her. Shireen couldn't speak, and there was no evidence that she understood what anyone was saying to her. Her brain damage was extensive and appalling… horrendous. On her behalf I felt angry.

If I went up to the ward and spoke to her, her head movement increased. But there was no way she could look at me, she was quite clearly blind. And because she didn't respond to any kind of visual stimulation, she scored very low on all kinds of occupational therapy tests. The tests were to try and gauge what level of functioning she was operating on, or how aware she was of the environment. A large part of those tests are to do with visual responses, tracking an object, responding to light… she didn't respond. She didn't cry, she didn't ever make any vocal sounds, never had tears, but I suspect that if she was in pain she thrashed about a bit more. I began to find her head movements expressive.

I found it hard at times to go on the ward and see her, because she was just so unreachable. I sometimes saw her relatives visiting her, touching her hand. They often seemed lost and unsure how to be with her. When nurses approached her, it was often to attend to her tubes or adjust her posture. Often people didn't know what to say. Her loneliness must have been unbelievable…. It was obvious…. Was she lonely? Did she know she was lonely?… I don't know.

I had quite a strong emotional sense about Shireen, whereas with some of the others on the ward it was quite different – it is difficult to admit this, but I would feel a sense of boredom, or a sense of being cut-off. At the same time, I felt a strong determination to 'find a way through' to reach them, although I must admit I almost despaired at times. But with Shireen, there seemed to be a lot going on inside her, and at the same time it seemed impossible for her to communicate it in any sort of meaningful way. I felt she was quite often in distress – her blindness bothered me – I wanted to touch her and give her some sense that I was there, and I didn't feel afraid to do that, although I'd usually tell her that I was going to touch her. I felt quite drawn to her…. With some people on the same ward I would be more careful of touching because they might experience this as quite startling. There was something about her that was warm….

It seems fairly likely that Shireen didn't understand language – I tried saying things that might be meaningful to her, like 'I saw your children came in yesterday'… and she didn't seem to show any change in response. But when she started coming to music therapy, she seemed to be listening! It was something to do with her head: that she was holding it very still, or that she was turning it towards the sound. Her face remained immobile… there was no change of expression.

The group

I saw Shireen in a music therapy group once a week for one hour, for two and a half years. There were three people in this group, and they were in quite a similar neurological state – and somehow working with three people seemed easier than working with one. It meant that in each group I needed to focus on one person for a certain amount of time, before moving on to the next. Then each person had some 'quality' time focused on them, but also some time when there was less focus, to listen and respond freely. I found that singing each person's name over and over again felt supportive and immediate. I would do this while improvising chords on the guitar.

I had a co-worker with me in the group, who was an occupational therapist. Each week, we would start the session by saying who we were, the date, the place, the time and even the year. Some group members might have impaired short-term memories, so it was important to give a sense of orientation. Then we would begin the musical greeting, which was always the same, to provide a sense of familiarity and also a sense of safety. The music would have spaces in it, to allow for people to respond, and it would focus very much on individual names, at that point in the session.

I would base the tempo of my guitar-playing and singing very much on the speed of someone's breathing pattern. So for example, in the greeting song, each verse would be absolutely related to something that this person was doing physically. If Shireen was moving her foot, then I would relate the speed of my playing to that, rather than to her breathing. What was strange was that I started to relate to her foot rather than to her whole body, and I almost started to put her personality into her foot! That was disconcerting and I'm glad I noticed it soon. The important thing was to take her in as a whole person – and this is difficult when you are sitting opposite someone who is in a tank of a wheelchair. Well, of course she needed something of that size and structure to support her posture and hold up her head. Because of her brain damage, her body was quite loose and floppy.

There were all sorts of instruments which I could put on her tray: the tray was part of her wheelchair, and it supported her arms. She responded a lot to a calabash – a light gourd about thirty centimetres high, with loosely tied beads around it. She would finger the beads and I would improvise something very quiet around that. I would play when she was playing, stop when she was stopping, just to try and make that contact with her.

There were various drums with different surfaces – a lovely Moroccan drum was very tautly stretched, and a tiny tap would produce ringing harmonics; a shaker made of Brazil nut shells, which she would feel and she could pick up. There were windchimes which I positioned on a long boom stand – and very soon I started to position them by her left foot, right down in front of her toes, so that if she did move her foot, then she would get feedback immediately from their ringing sound. And every week she did make some sounds – it took two or three months before I had any sense that she was doing it purposefully.... And then over the weeks, she started to do things like playing only when I was singing, and when the singing stopped she would put her foot back on her footplate. Then she started doing things like moving her foot right along the windchimes and then kicking out as well. She was really experimenting!

By this time our department had purchased another set of windchimes. It seemed so important that she could have those down by her foot all the time in the sessions. We needed another set for other group members to play if they chose.

A new relationship

What started to happen over two years of work was that she was getting more and more involved; she was finding more ways of playing with her foot, and relating to the music in a different way. She started to link up musically with another person in the group, Paul. He had some kind of cerebellar degeneration and was slowly losing his cognitive and physical skills. But he had reliable movement with his elbow: he was able to move from his shoulder, move it up and down. The co-worker would hold a keyboard underneath his elbow and he would play on the keyboard, able to control the music quite well. Paul was a very emotional person and cried and laughed a lot – he was very expressive considering his very limiting cognitive and physical disabilities. Although Shireen couldn't see him, she must have been able to hear where he was. In the group improvisations, I would generally play something quite continuous so that the music kept going. The people in the group couldn't necessarily aim to play at a particular point, as they didn't have that physical control, but they could join in at any time. They had very distinctive sounding instruments so that it was noticeable who was playing at any one time. What started to happen was that Shireen would play and then Paul, then Shireen again, and so on. I didn't notice this during the session, but noticed it when I was listening to the tapes of sessions. It began to happen too much for it to be a coincidence.

What I had not expected was that there was a group awareness. These were three very cut-off people who were beginning to communicate with each other! This was, of course, the purpose of the group, but at first it felt that I was working with three individuals, and there was little sense of a group feeling. The third member, Frank, was nearly always asleep. Because of his brain damage he could not always remain alert. But when he was awake he was fantastic! He had quite a lot of movement with his hands and used to play the autoharp beautifully, with long strums and little ones and amazing musical intelligence. It was always worth having him in the group, though, giving him that opportunity just in case he was awake... so in a way he was an absent member of the group. But Paul and Shireen became increasingly interactive. It must have been the first relationship that Shireen developed after her brain injury....

She would have nurses dressing and undressing her, removing tubes – and they would talk her through every procedure. But we had this feeling that she didn't understand... we all kept talking to her but it was easy to lack conviction because there really was no evidence that she understood. At times I lacked conviction too, but I didn't have any doubt about the importance of the music. I felt that my music was communicating with her. In speaking with her I used to think, why am I saying this – there *is* a value in her hearing my voice, and the musical side of my voice... but the actual content of the words I wasn't sure about... she'd never done anything I'd asked her to do like 'could you squeeze my hand?' Perhaps she didn't understand, or perhaps she did but was unable to act on the suggestion. Then again, perhaps she didn't want to. There is always the power one has by refusing – and why should she want to do that, squeeze my hand?

And yet, I had a sense of her personality. I really noticed her absence if she wasn't there – in fact she hardly ever missed a session, only once she was ill, and once when her family visited. I felt that she got a deep sense of peace from the music, her breathing was often more relaxed at the end of sessions.

I found it difficult at times, deciding on what kind of music to play in the group, what kind of mood to offer. The only way that seemed to me to have integrity was to ask myself 'what is the feeling in this group today?'... and then play music that related to the feeling in some way. I needed to be aware of what feelings *I* had before going into the group. If I were to bring my *own* feelings into the group, then it would not be therapeutic for others! The job could be incredibly stressful at times, so I had to work especially hard not to bring my own stresses into the group setting.

But if I went into a session and became aware of new emotions which did not seem to be related to any experience I'd had that day, then these feelings might well have been transferred by the group members themselves. To some extent I was able to use this 'counter-transference' to become more in touch with how the people in the group were feeling, and I could put this into the music. Supervision helped me to sort out what feelings belonged where and to whom – because I think that I have my own despair when confronted with someone who actually has been very much like you or me, living a normal existence and then lost so much, so that my own grief would have got caught up in it.

I always had to cope with the fact that I am the main provider of the notes... that was quite hard, but once I decided to take on that responsibility, then I had to be brave, go into the void and say 'here is some music'. But the music had to be orientating, it had to start to divide time up, it had to be structured and structuring otherwise we were all lost!

In the group improvisations, I tried to provide a structured rhythmic support through my playing and singing, and at the same time, to respond to the moment. I provided music that is stable, long and ongoing. The group had a lot of time to practice coordinating their movements, and I was beginning to feel that when they did play, it was on significant beats. I had to provide the pulse, and therefore the grid of sound. I could then respond to them immediately in terms of volume or sound texture, in fact, in terms of anything that I could possibly musically reflect, imitate or acknowledge. I had to feed off all the cues I could because I wanted that music to be part of their experience rather than me just bringing something new and imposing. I really wanted to be commenting, through music, on what was going on. So if someone breathed more heavily, then that would immediately change my playing. It was as though I was some kind of cipher: I was receiving and offering music – it was *our* music, not just mine imposed on to the group.

There were times in sessions when there was just silence. Sometimes, no music began... but then, occasionally, there might be a sound from someone. At times, group members became agitated in the silence – it became too painful – and then I would start some continuous music.

Leaving

At times I wondered whether Shireen wanted to be alive – and I don't know how aware she was. I was not always sure whether she was there, present in the sessions. But she always came – for two and a half years, for an hour every week. What I noticed was that she started to show increased facial expression. The change in her was so incredibly gradual... it took two years before I'd say she'd smiled – but there were hints of a smile for quite a long time before.... On the whole, the hardest thing was having to cope with not knowing, not being sure of what was going on for her, in her mind, in the sessions.

After the group had been running for two years, I decided to move to another part of the country. I managed to negotiate a ten-week leaving period – although four weeks is the usual length of time to give notice. This gave me more time to say goodbye to the group – I felt that I couldn't possibly wind up in four weeks! I found the ending especially difficult for this group – we had been together for such a long time! In this session, I told the group that I was going to leave. Paul started crying. The music was so much more charged than usual – I want to play you the tape of this session.

> Cathy's playing on the guitar is firm and steady, and Shireen sounds strong on the wind chimes. Cathy is singing non-verbally, accompanied by a guitar chord sequence. I hear Paul on the cymbal... he starts to sing... the music is filled with emotion, the sound is full... and then a high-pitched sound seems to come from nowhere. It is a long sound, an arc, an aaaaaaaaaaaaaaahhh! over the music, over everything else.

That cry! That is Shireen! And she'd never made a sound before, never in our whole two years of working! She just cried out... I was so thrown that I hit a wrong note on the guitar. In that moment, I suddenly knew that she had some sense of something... it was too much of a coincidence... the fact that she cried, the way that she was playing... we all carried on playing, on and on, we didn't want the music to stop. After that, it was time for the goodbye song and neither of them would play.

I continued with the group for another nine weeks. Paul and Shireen were angry, which was so necessary. The worst thing would have been if

I had said, 'I'm going' and there was no response... I'd have thought they were totally resigned, or they didn't understand, or the group meant very little to them. But Paul and Shireen were very angry, and for about four weeks they refused to play. After that they gradually became more musically involved in terms of making sounds, and it felt as if there was a kind of acceptance.

But her cry! That moves me very deeply every time I hear it, and I have played that tape quite a number of times... it is as though Shireen is right there, in the room.

I now wonder what kind of experience she'd had of trying to communicate, and of people just not being able to pick this up at all. Maybe her foot moving all the time *was* her only purposeful communication... and people were saying, 'she's moving her foot but she seems to be doing it randomly, so therefore I don't think it is important...'! And maybe it *was* just random, but maybe it wasn't, maybe she was trying to communicate, and in the end, if communication is not recognized, one just gives up!

People who have any insight at all into their condition following profound brain injury are at risk of becoming depressed, for obvious reasons. Often, as people begin to recover their faculties slightly, they become more aware of their situation and therefore more withdrawn. That can be a sign that they are beginning to recover. I do wonder whether Shireen 'knew' or 'felt' her situation; I even wonder whether she was able to conceptualize it. She must have felt *some* sense of loss.... In the work we did together, I listened to her and hopefully gave her a chance to feel more like a human being, and to receive some emotional support. I hope that music gave her the experience that her own feelings were being acknowledged in some way.

Coda

Music therapy can be a setting where people express their despair. They can also experience optimism, and express it... people can just do what they want, and not be given instructions. And there is no need for language. At times some music therapy groups seem to have very little happening in them – but invariably something happens the following week. It is important with very slow therapy like this to keep going, to have consistency and not cancel the group. At times it is hard to keep going....

I don't work there anymore. One reason is that I felt I was almost starting to get used to that situation, and this felt like not a good thing... even a little dangerous. Doing this work has made me aware of the quality of living, and that it is possible to have a really close time with someone who is extremely disabled. Sometimes one feels a strong sense of love, and very much in contact.

The work has made me much more aware of a kind of fight in people. In some there is a fight, a desire to live despite all the odds. I have also seen some people so restricted that I have wondered whether it is worth them being alive.... Some quite clearly don't want to be alive and have no option... and I think that is absolute hell.

I shall not be quite the same again... this work has changed my views and feelings about taking and giving life.... So I would say to other music therapists, at times this is very isolating work, but so very worthwhile.

And take care of yourself.

Reflections

Whose feelings?

How does Cathy know what to do with Shireen in music therapy? How does she manage to continue working with her for two and a half years? How does she stop herself from becoming totally overwhelmed by Shireen's loneliness, the loss of her family, the baby she has never known, the loss of her faculties? Does Shireen exist? Do any of us exist when we cannot see, hear, feel, taste? Do we exist when we don't know that we exist?

In this story, Cathy enters into Shireen's world. A world in which music therapy – or anything for that matter – may or may not make any impression on this being, trapped inside a body. Shireen's foot movements seem to be haphazard, and there are no tests appropriate to her condition. She scores low or nil. It takes months of music therapy before Cathy begins to suspect that Shireen's foot-sounds on the windchimes may not be haphazard after all. And even then, Cathy has no way of checking: she can only believe. And go by her feelings.

Her feelings about Shireen are warm, despite no overt reciprocity from Shireen. Cathy wants her to know that she is there, that she cares, that she wants to know her, to touch her and somehow let her know that she is not alone. Cathy hears, knows, has a sense of Shireen. Where does this sensing come from? Cathy does not feel these feeling for other people on the ward, or even with other music therapy clients – with some, she speaks of having quite different feelings: of feeling numb at times, bored, dead... why and how does she feel warmth for Shireen? Is it Shireen's warmth that she experiences, or her own? Is the quality of warmth that Cathy feels for Shireen different from the quality of her own, personal warmth that she experiences with other people? Could it be that Cathy receives feelings from Shireen – feelings that Shireen herself does not 'know' – and responds to these with a warmth that has a particular quality: the quality that is the combination of who Cathy and Shireen are, as individual persons *and* in relation to one another?

Cathy explains some of her 'knowing' of Shireen in terms of *counter-transference*. In any therapeutic encounter, the client develops feelings towards the therapist. These feelings, called *transference*, were identified by Freud as having more to do with the client's own past relationships – perhaps with parents – than with the client's relationship with the therapist. The client brings the past into the present, through transference. The therapist becomes aware of these feelings, and responds to them. The therapist's feelings, in response to the client's, are known as counter-transference. With therapeutic training comes the knowledge and understanding that counter-transference is an important clinical tool: it enables the therapist to gain insights into the client, into what the client is saying (and not saying) and feeling (and not feeling). In music therapy, transference and counter-transference may happen within the music (e.g. how the therapist and the patient actually play music together, what the client's music evokes in the therapist's music); it may 'cross-over' between music and feelings (e.g. what feelings the client experiences as a result of improvising certain music together with the therapist, or what the therapist feels in response to the client's playing); and transference and counter-transference happen non-musically (e.g. through a complex mixture of words, movements, facial expression, posture, and so on). An important aspect of any therapeutic work is that the therapist shares insights gained as a result of counter-transference with the patient – either through talking, playing music, or through 'being with' the patient in a certain way. And also watches, listens, feels closely for a response from the patient.

But Shireen cannot hear, cannot see, cannot know, cannot respond. She has no posture, facial expression, verbal or vocal sounds to help Cathy experience her. And, as far as we can tell, Shireen does not seem to 'conceptualize' feelings – it seems that she might not even feel feelings – she might, rather, feel unformed fragments that still manage to communicate themselves to Cathy, and to which Cathy can respond: she resonates, inwardly, with Shireen's feelings. And because of her training, Cathy manages to gain some clarity as to where these come from, and allow herself to work warmly and intimately with this intensely lonely woman. She can feel Shireen's feelings on her behalf, and have fun with her! Rather than being only overwhelmed by Shireen's pathology.

These very complex emotional issues can be explored in clinical supervision. Music therapists (and indeed most therapists) consult colleagues on a regular basis, for 'supervision'. Supervision means that someone 'accompanies' music therapists on their journeys with patients. Cathy talks to her supervisor about feelings that she has, about things that she does not understand, about work situations that frustrate her, and this talking with her supervisor can help bring about some clarity, complexity and richness of meaning to what goes on in music therapy. In her supervision sessions, Cathy learns to 'check' her own feelings: which feelings belong to music therapy with Shireen, and which do not. Once she can do that, she can be fairly certain that her feelings for Shireen are – in some mysterious way – in response to Shireen's own feelings towards her, Cathy. She can also 'leave aside' feelings that are not part of her work with Shireen, so that these do not bring 'emotional clutter' to the musical space.

Tuning-in

Cathy has an awesome responsibility: to provide music for three clients who are physically passive, and at the same time to not impose her own music on to the group. As the only member of the group who can play, she faces a musical void: Shireen, Frank and Paul sit in silence, with little movement that might give Cathy cues of tempo, phrasing, or rhythm, that she can transform into music. Within this void, Cathy needs to provide music that is appropriate to everyone in the group.

How would Cathy impose music on to the group session? Let us imagine that, for whatever reason, Cathy feels frustrated. The quality of her frustration is somewhat tight, she feels rushed. There are at least two possibilities here. Cathy can choose to not tune-in to the group, she can play her own music, rather lively and faster than usual – let's call it 'frustrated' music. If the group were able to respond, then the members might join in, and tune-in to her 'frustrated' music with its faster tempo and tighter playing. This might well take them out of their own passivity, and they might enjoy this rather lively music – and everyone might have an enlivening session. But here we need to ask ourselves: who is the music for? And whose music is it? Is it Cathy's own, exclusive music, which will just have to do for today? Is the music *only* for the group members? And what about Cathy? Is Cathy not *also* part of the group?

Another possibility is that Cathy ignores her frustration, and manages to play music that is not tight or fast. And here we might ask ourselves whether this music is authentic. Is it really coming from her? Can she tune-in to the group, which includes *her*, if she is not acknowledging her own music for the sake of being 'professional'?

The musical void and physical passivity of this group leaves these questions exposed – and lonely. And indeed, Cathy speaks of the loneliness of this work. She simply does not know, at times, whether the music is 'right' or not. A more active group would help her – would help everyone – to tune-in, by being more overtly part of the music, by altering any rhythm or tempo or phrasing that did not feel part of their own, personal music. Here, Cathy has to 'provide' the music. Alone.

The clinical intention of her music is that it includes *all* group members; that it reflects something of their own tempo, rhythm, phrasing, and energy, and galvanizes them towards some kind of presence in the session – even if the patients are not able to show their presence through musical acts. Cathy describes the music she plays as marking time, structuring the world, as providing a grid, a predictable and flexible environment of sound that can go on and on and on. The fact that she is improvising 'live' music rather than playing a recording means that she has the flexibility to adapt her playing instantly to acknowledge Shireen, Paul or Frank's tiniest in-breath, sound or movement. This allows each of the three group members time and space to join in the music, in their own time, and to resonate with the music and become part of it – even if only in their minds and in their invisible, unknowable feelings.

Earlier in this book we spoke of the psycho-neurological phenomenon of *entrainment*, where any biological being begins to 'fit in' with the environment, by synchronizing with the rhythm, speed, vibration and energy of the environment. Cathy's music provides an environment which is almost in slow motion: music that is steady enough, for long enough, to allow even these three people whose brains are severely damaged, to begin to entrain with the musical environment in their own way and in their own time. This entrainment may only happen inwardly, leaving Cathy with no visible or audible cue that the members are, in fact, tuning-in to the music. The slow, steady and flexible music allows Shireen, Paul and Frank to tune-in *for themselves* – this is crucial in their condition – and in their own time. They are given the space to play music, to respond, to be present in the music even if they do not have the cognitive, perceptual or physical capacity to make this decision.

Despite their deep neurological damage, Shireen, Paul and Frank can be a *part of* a living musical experience that includes Cathy and the co-worker. The group music improvisation respects and addresses their distinctive and precious humanity – and binds *all* the persons in the music therapy group together.

CHAPTER 8

Miriam and Seaun
Danger and Intimacy in a Secure Unit[1]

The settings

I went straight from music therapy training at the Guildhall into my first job – I wanted to work in psychiatry. My first job was in Brixton, London – I took the tube there, came out of the station and the whole feeling was volatile. Life on the streets seemed only just contained.... I had never been exposed to that, I hadn't lived in London, I'd only heard of Brixton spoken of in hushed tones... its riots... but something in me wanted to conquer my being terrified of that kind of thing... and on the acute wards, people seemed really disturbed. I was terrified.

Forensic psychiatry means that you work primarily with mentally disordered offenders. Everybody has a criminal history, or has become unmanageable in general psychiatric services. Some have committed crimes and while in prison have become mentally ill. At that point they are transferred to a psychiatric unit, one which is secure and meets prison requirements. There are also people who commit a crime during a psychotic episode: they may have been suffering from a paranoid delusion at the time, and you have to ask, did they kill somebody because they were paranoid? Because they feared that this person was going to kill them? A lot of our patients fall into this category, and forensic work demands an awareness of how the legal system impacts on patient care.

1   Based on the interview with Claire Hobbs. Claire works in acute and forensic psychiatry in London.

Then there are the psychopaths, and they are regarded as the most incurable of all forensic patients. Psychopaths basically have no sense of responsibility to themselves or other people. They tend to act out impulses directly, with no apparent thought between the impulse and the action. They appear to have no sense of right and wrong, and have no remorse for their often violent or aggressive actions. They tend to go to higher security services than ours. I worked on the acute and on the locked wards.

The Unit runs an assessment programme for new people, for four to six weeks, and music therapy is part of this. People come to music therapy groups, and are asked to commit themselves to coming for those first four weeks as this gives me a chance to get to know them, and for them to get to know what music therapy is about. Most people find the sessions fun. I always take them to the room, show them around and explain the idea of music therapy to them.

The music therapy room is quite large, about five by five metres, and I have all sorts of instruments set out. I have a big xylophone, a metallophone, an Indian double headed drum, an orchestral gong, cymbals, conga drums, bongos, temple blocks, gato drum, small timpani drum, a bigger timpani type drum, a clavinova – which means I can see people. Whereas with a piano you tend to have your back to some people, and with those who are unpredictable that is not satisfactory. Then there is a whole collection of small instruments, a thumb piano, cabassa (rattle with beads outside), shakers, woodblocks, pan pipes, recorder, tambourines, and so on.

When I started working here, I thought I could be very non-directive, just allow to happen what would happen in the group sessions. I quickly realized that many of the patients are so lost, they don't know how to communicate in any way, they don't know how to use music to communicate, let alone how to use music as a metaphor. They are often hard to motivate in the first place, so I started to think about how to get them engaged in the sessions. Some have been locked away for such a long time that they have lost self-motivation and autonomy. I had to make a real effort to get them involved and interested by quite structured means – structuring sessions in such a way that I could then engage them in more long-term and insightful work.

In the group sessions we do various things. For example, each person has a chance to play anything they like on their own, and then we can use this as a basis for talking about listening to each other, about how we all need to feel heard, how we need to hear what other people do. Or I might start playing and each person joins in one by one. Each time someone joins in, they listen to what the two or three people before them are doing so that they become aware of the sounds that are around before they add their voice to it... that usually works well. Once this is established, I might start to play slowly, fast, loudly, quietly – or I might play instruments in an unconventional way – brushing the top of a drum for instance – and see how people respond. And we talk about how anything that I did influenced what everybody else did, and how much people are listening and how they can respond to what somebody else does.

I constantly check that patients understand what I am saying – and this doesn't have to be patronising but I must make sure they know, because if they don't know, they go away and won't come back. Occasionally people say 'this is a load of nonsense' – and I encourage them to listen really hard and try to take in what is going on in the music rather than focusing on the more superficial chaotic sound which often emerges. I've become firmer in dealing with those kinds of comments. Then I'll suggest that somebody tries to influence everybody in the group through their playing. If that works I can suggest people reflect on what it feels like being in control of the group and getting people to do whatever they want. This is often a way in for people. We talk about how being here, in the unit, feels terrible and everyone else is in control of what you are doing: doctors, prison warders, nurses... and by playing music like this, you get a feel of how much fun it is to be in charge – and usually people do pick this up. For the rest of the session, we might play freely and look at how the music reflects our moods – and I encourage people to think about different kinds of music. So for example, when they listen to music, sometimes they want to listen to energetic music, other times to sad music, and that depends on their mood. We talk about this and it makes sense to everyone.

Miriam

Very often, women on the secure unit have personality disorders and seem to be the hardest of people to work with. They are often intensely manipulative. None of the women will engage in music therapy at the moment, apart from one.

Miriam is from Uganda. She said she was twenty, but we didn't know her age. She had become a refugee over there, with no knowledge of her mother or father, and had been farmed out to look after local children. She'd had a close relationship with her grandmother who died when she was about eight or nine. She'd then been sent for by a relation in England, and came over when she was thirteen, speaking no English. She'd gone to school for a while, but had always been intensely isolated. Then she got into a relationship which appears to have been very abusive, and had a baby when she was about seventeen. She killed the child (a girl) when she was three. It was on a Sunday last June, she smothered it because she felt that life was unbearable both for her and the child. She then planned to kill herself, had tried three times and failed, and after the third attempt she was found and taken to hospital.

She was charged with killing her child, sent to prison, was there for a week but was too depressed and was a major suicide risk so she was transferred to the Unit. This was only three weeks after the event. She said nothing, she looked dreadful. I returned to work after a break in September, about two months after she got there, and by this time she was willing to do anything to relieve boredom. When you think about her cultural background and her whole life, she'd had no consistent care-giver, she'd been a refugee from when she was virtually a baby, and was then uprooted to a country far removed from the culture of her childhood. Here was someone who had lived in a very small village with a feeling that everybody is your family and you help everybody else ... and had then been dumped in this cold climate, in a culture where people don't generally relate like that!

Miriam was a bright woman, very able – and her child hadn't been buried by the end of September. There'd been a long inquest, and part of the whole process of working with her on the Unit was to try and encourage some kind of grieving for her child.

In the group music therapy sessions she used music instinctively: she could make connections between music and herself, she used it to communicate with people, and what she played influenced them in the music. I pointed these things out to her and she became more and more confident. What first struck me in the music therapy group was that she would play something to somebody and expect a response – this was an instinctive 'this is what music is for'. Hers was not an isolated, uncommunicative unrelating playing at all. In one session, when we were doing an exercise playing something to influence other people, she was playing quite a small instrument in many different ways. It was as though she was playing a game and enjoying it – there was this spark of enthusiasm for life in her – and this is relatively rare in this setting. And I thought,

> you don't seem to be psychiatrically ill, emotionally disconnected – you are deeply affected by everything that has happened to you, and all your natural instincts are just there – and nobody has really given you the opportunity to be this – you don't know how to make relationships with people in this culture, you don't know how to find help or find people who've been through similar experiences, but... you're not mad.

That is what I thought, through experiencing her playing in music therapy groups.

I think she knew that I recognized that she wasn't mad – and it was not only me, but others in the team also began to build up relationships with her. I never had to explain things twice – I could use any words I wanted; I could talk to her as if she were somebody I knew, at my level, and she would understand... but if you talked to her as if she were a disabled hospital patient, you'd drive her further into a kind of isolation. In the music therapy group she found a voice.

The whole team started to get to what had really happened, what had led up to her killing her child. She did not have a personality disorder – it was a reactive depression – I don't think that she was even given a psychiatric label in the end: it really was caused by intense stress and the prison sentence was dropped.

Miriam was rare in that setting, because she didn't present a danger to the public. She had committed a crime and needed psychiatric care, and because at the time she was still under the prison system, she wouldn't have been allowed to go to an open ward... so she ended up here at the Unit.

Her grieving process started to happen, and the debate began as to whether she wanted to go to the child's funeral. But really at that stage she was still so much in shock... the trauma was still too new. She wanted to make a cross for the child's grave in woodwork... this became very important: it was part of her coming to terms with, and acknowledging the child as dead. And then, with what seemed like little preparation, she was transferred to an open ward – a bed became available – and we weren't told. She was here, with us, and then suddenly she was gone – and that was very sad. There was no chance to go to see her and to evaluate our input.

I don't know what has happened to her now... this is one of the intensely frustrating things: people get transferred, and there is no more contact... so the relationships that we create are just taken away. From them and from us.

Caring, fear and evil

Often, forensic patients draw out a caring part of me. They are like desperately lost children, so very often. The first thing we think of when a new patient comes in is, is it safe? We read the history – we usually know the index offence – so we know what someone has done. And we all do have this curiosity about the macabre... we have to find out what someone has done, how could they do that... perhaps it is the fear of knowing that we have those kind of impulses in us; these intensely destructive, aggressive impulses, but we wouldn't dream of being anything other than well behaved. For me to lose my temper is rare! There is a curiosity to meet the person who has done this, and when I do meet them, I often think 'he's pathetic, he looks weak, he looks sad...' and yet there is still this kind of fear: he could do that to me.

I have a music therapy group at the moment – they are all rapists. Two of those are intensely charming people and don't arouse any real fear in me – I know everything they have done, I know their history – and I now know that the fact that they don't arouse any real fear in me is their most frightening aspect. They are charming so they could easily draw me in – that is how they manage to rape people, because nobody has been suspicious, no one has felt frightened in their company. Whereas the third member of that group never says anything openly, he makes all sorts innuendoes, he never makes eye contact with me at all. And he brings out this kind of chill in me – because there is nothing you can talk about: you cannot talk about what he has done, he denies it altogether and has done several times.... I don't know whether he is aware of the effect he has on me. I feel chilled with him.

Sometimes I think that I am idealistic in thinking that destructiveness is an expression of something, or that it is connected to a lack of love in earlier life. Bad exists. I know that, this is it, here.... There is a man at the moment who I've seen in groups... he killed a seven-month-old baby, six months ago, poured bleach down its throat. It was his girlfriend's baby, not his. Having done that he then put a knife down the baby's throat and twisted the knife. It is so sadistic, even some of the doctors did not want to go and see him. After a few weeks we were told we must see him, make contact with him. He's a tiny man, very weedy, but he has very hard eyes. I look at him and think 'do I see a murderer when I look at you?' I do. I don't see somebody sad or ill. I can't make any contact with him, he sneers at everything I say, he is very articulate... and I actually think this is evil, and I want to avoid him, I don't want to work with him, I am glad when he doesn't come to me. That is rare. I do feel some apprehension occasionally about certain people turning up for sessions, but on the whole I am glad when they come, and am satisfied when I've had a reasonable session with them. But him I don't want to see.

In this work, when you actually first feel that fear, you know you are really involved: it is not just an exterior curiosity. Your own fear is an essential tool in assessing the risk of those patients, in fact, it is a clinical tool: fear is the counter-transference, and it tells you something about the person, it helps you to know how you can work with them. As long as your fear is controlled, and you know where it belongs, then it is manageable. It is very important to understand when fear is imagined and when it is real, and that you don't act on the imagined, because then you put up yet another block for that patient. If you are paranoid about them, you will not really help them. You've got to get to a level where you still feel safe within yourself, but at the same time you need to understand what it feels like to be afraid....

I think there is a tolerance limit, though. And I know that when I start to feel low, then I start to think that everybody in the world is like that; there is so much bad about... I start to feel paranoid about the world around me.

There is another overwhelming feeling that I experience in the Unit, and that is one of timidity. It is as if these people who have been so 'bad' are intensely frightened for themselves. And maybe this is why you never get this feeling of intimacy in the work, because they are just so afraid of it, they hold back.... And I have experienced this concreteness often in forensic work. People focus on 'what is this instrument made of, where does it come from, how is it put together'... if you focus on its physical properties, then you don't have to see the instrument as representing something, as expressing anything directly; you don't have to see its potential for beauty, for making music, for self-expression.

Some of the patients here are intensely self-destructive: people who cut themselves constantly, people who do things you'd never imagine anyone doing – and I sit in a room with a whole lot of sticks, and I sometimes think I have a lot of weapons in this room. But whatever is destructive can also be used creatively, and retaining faith in that is important. Here, I make music with some of the most destructive people I will probably ever meet. And they express such a love for music, an enthusiasm for music – particularly the Afro-Caribbean guys, they are often fantastic drummers! I feel optimistic for them when I hear how much they love playing. But I also wonder that when they don't engage in music therapy, perhaps they don't actually want to contaminate something that they love so much... with the part of them that they hate so much. People feel contaminated by their deeds, and they don't want to contaminate something that they love.

When working with patients we always wear alarms, and there is usually another member of staff in the music therapy group. If they are going to be away then I always make sure that there is someone in the room next door, in the office, when I am working. One of the things that I feel safe with, and that is also unrealistic, is that in this environment everything is quite controlled and secure. I have an alarm. I've never used it but have accidentally set it off – and there is a team of people who respond, and they are there within twenty seconds. They are so fast! And this is not real life. If this were out on the street, I wouldn't be wearing the alarm – I wouldn't even approach someone like these patients, let alone talk to them....

I also think that fear is something inside me that I want to get through, for myself, for the work. Because I believe that everybody can be creative... when the music comes in, it can reach everybody, there is some hope in this person, he is still alive, he is still here, he still wants to get out, he has some faith in life. I want to get through that block of fear to be able to work creatively with people.

Seaun

Seaun is about thirty, he's had a fairly disruptive background, split-up parents, lots of truanting from school, he ran away from a step-father when he was sixteen and then lived alone. He shared flats with friends, had various odd jobs, had some training in computing, plays the guitar, and basically slipped into an existence of lots of street drugs, busking, hanging around... when he was in his mid twenties he raped a woman at knifepoint in the East End at about ten at night... he may have been suffering from a drug-induced psychosis. He was charged and transferred to an interim secure unit, was then moved out to a private hospital, and transferred back to the secure unit two years ago. After that he showed symptoms of a fairly long-term psychotic illness and a personality disorder, and has been on anti-psychotic medication for some years now.

I have seen Seaun in three separate periods. He came for an assessment group and sat around and played Bob Dylan songs on the guitar. He let other people join him, was quite interactive but focused on playing the guitar, which he could do. That was over a period of two months. I then suggested that he move into a closed music therapy group, that he commit himself to coming regularly, which he did. He seemed to be manic at that stage: he would play very loudly for very long periods and then talk incessantly. I remember actually stopping him in mid-flow once, and saying 'stop talking, stay quiet for a moment and try to listen to other people, because this group will be destructive if people don't listen to each other'. And he did – he responded to firm talking to – which I had to do to set boundaries.

He gradually became very withdrawn and then stopped coming altogether. I went to him and asked him to come, as he contributed so much to the sessions. His only response was 'No I'm useless' and walked out… that was the last time he actually spoke to any of us. That was in the January, and I went away from March until September of that year. While I was away, he went through this period of being verbally aggressive to the staff. They were testing him out for re-engaging with therapy programmes. At that stage he was making some inappropriate comments to all the women… very sexual comments – and they wouldn't let any of the women work with him – and most of us are women!

He asked me whether he could come to music therapy again, and eventually the team agreed. He has been coming for the past three months, as part of a group, and what has struck me is the difference between when he comes on his own – because the others don't turn up – and when he is with the other group members.

When he is the only one who arrives for sessions, we have long improvisations, with him taking the lead either on guitar, drums, xylophone or whatever, and me joining in with him. He seems to know what he wants to do, and it can be something very simple: he once played a beautiful, very simple chord pattern on the guitar. He kept playing it for about fifteen minutes, and I made variations on this at the piano. Then he moved to the temple blocks and played a rhythm which included beating the guitar strings – it was very effective. Then he went back to the guitar and changed his tune altogether – from the major chords he went into a minor, and I played the recorder and wove this tune around his playing. There was this extraordinary feeling of intimacy, of knowing where each other is, and of having met each other…. I said something to him about that, and he said 'that was really beautiful I really enjoyed that' and then he kept very quiet on the way back to the ward. He wouldn't talk about it any more once we'd left the room. It was as if he knew that once he was outside that room he had to be the patient again, and had to talk to me in a very careful way. That intimacy could not exist anywhere but in that room, in music.

When other members of the group came for sessions, he seemed to struggle. In the beginning, he would give up trying to be part of the group and become withdrawn, almost as though he didn't know how to fit in. In one session, one particular guy just played this incessant rhythm for fifty minutes... we all tried to break in, and Seaun was trying too – and eventually he gave up, and the other person just carried on. Seaun gave up completely. And this would happen when the others took over, he would just withdraw, give up – as if he had lost both intimacy and autonomy in the group. And it was also as though he'd lost control and influence over his life in general, rather than just in the group.

But gradually, over the past weeks, he has become more able to assert himself. Like one week, it was about our fifth session, the others all came, and he played the guitar. I asked whether he wanted to start off and he did quite a strong rhythmic strumming and the others joined in with him. They had to pick up his rhythm because it was so clear. He led the others with this chord pattern that everyone could join in with easily and he seemed able to contain the whole group. It was as though he had translated his own instinct into 'I can fit with other people as well.... I can make other people do things the way that I want to do them.... I don't have to completely be a victim to their patterns'... he was surprised at how effective he was... his face lit up. He has quite a mobile, expressive face. At another session, he got together a few drums, built his own drum kit – I think he took something from under someone's nose – and set up an invigorating rhythmic pattern – and again the others joined in with him. He was suddenly finding that he had this ability to lead other people. He seemed pleased and surprised by this!

He missed a few sessions because of medical appointments – he seemed disappointed when he missed sessions – and when I told the group that I was going to be on holiday he said, 'God, that's a racket!' He seemed disappointed and annoyed. He asked me several times, that session and the next, what date I was going to be back on – it was as if he'd suddenly registered that I was going to be away, and when was I going to be back. Then he went into this complete dream, the session had a disappointed feeling – and I have always felt that with him when a session is shortened or missed for any reason… and that is where we've left it.

Every time we have had musical intimacy between us, he has been on his own. In an extraordinary way, it is as deep an intimacy as I've had in that setting. When there is a group of people, though, he finds it very difficult – but he is finding a way: when he takes it upon himself, he can really lead, he can do it. His personality seems… dreamy, spaced out… it is not a natural thing for him to be assertive.

Legalizing security

An enormous complication in this work is that the legal system is involved with every aspect of the patient. Sometimes, you are dealing with patients who have a separate agenda. For example, someone who is serving a prison sentence and has then been transferred to hospital may have no real investment in being mentally well enough to return to prison. Some people prefer prison, they say they know where they are in prison – but once you go back to prison you have to serve your sentence. Some patients have a vested interest in not engaging in therapy, in remaining ill: this means that they might not go back to prison, and will eventually be discharged directly into the community. There are one or two with whom we suspect faked symptoms, which is very difficult to deal with. Others know that their discharge from hospital back into the community is dependent on a good Home Office report, and all patients know that we all contribute to the report. These patients are keen that we show them to be no risk to the public… they have to be 'safe'.

What we never know is how doctors interpret what we write. There is a tendency to be over-cautious, and treat every 'normal' expression of aggression as pathological – and that is very scary. Something can be taken out of context and acted on rather severely, and this gives the patient little faith in ordinary common sense. We all know that forensic patients are, to the public, highly dangerous, and if anything were to happen, there is an enormous backlash which could reflect on the doctor responsible for the whole case… and so there is a tendency to act with great caution in every case. It is often so hard to get patients to express and to acknowledge that aggression exists – it is natural, it is frightening, it exists in all of us, and music can help to begin to express something that is in all of us.

And every time I get close to somebody, that is the time when they shut down. People are constantly guarded, they can feel watched, paranoid about the whole system, but the system is set up to make them feel even more paranoid. They feel reported on at every moment, and this is a dilemma – they are stuck here. It is not just their paranoia as a result of their illness, but they feel a very real paranoia about everything being recorded. You can even feel it as a staff member: everybody knows where you are all the time – they have to, in a way, but you still feel it. Everything you write is scrutinized – so you have to be very, very careful about what you write. If you give any hint that somebody is dangerous it will be explored further.

All this can be intensely frustrating and depressing – I experience a tension at times, that nothing I do is really effective. I cannot speak my mind either to the patient or in my feedback to colleagues, I cannot say what has really happened....

Through music I have a belief in goodness and healthiness in the most damaged of people. There is spirituality in music in itself – and I occasionally feel this, even working in such difficult circumstances. And then I think it is worth while.

Reflections

On patterns and patterning

Claire describes her first impressions of Brixton, London, as being 'only just contained' – the streets feel volatile, as though they might get out of control, explode at any moment. In contrast to this is the secure unit, where every aspect of life is tightly controlled: days are structured, staff carry alarms, patients are 'observed'. There is little risk, here, of volatility.

In each of these scenarios we can reflect on the forming and unforming of patterns – and of how they feel. The streets of Brixton have their own kind of pattern – not formal or even that noticeable, but

Claire is able to describe the street as a *whole* – her experience is a unified one, a fusion of her senses and capacity to perceive the sounds, smells, shapes as going together. In musical terms we can imagine what Claire sees, smells, hears and feels as music: contours of sounds and shapes, rhythms of smells and colours, the dynamic/volume levels of sounds, of people rushing, being still or meandering, the harmony or discord of how the street 'feels'. Although all of these belong together, and she experiences them as one, her impression is that this 'one' has an undertow of instability. The streets feel threatening: the place is unfamiliar and she senses a frightening fragility. Things might 'fall apart'. In other words, the pattern might change. Her unease, though, is about *how* this pattern might change. Her intuition is that it might change very suddenly into something unknown, something different – the streets might explode towards sudden chaos. Chaos that may last, or else quickly settle into a different pattern. In contrast, the Unit that she describes has a pattern of stability – it almost feels a dead pattern: deeply entrenched, and any hint of moving beyond, or even, perhaps, of getting a feel for the pattern's shape and boundaries, is swiftly dealt with. Staff carry alarms and there is an emergency response team. Twenty seconds.

Let's take this scenario into the music therapy group.

In the group sessions, Claire first attempts to be 'non-directive'; in other words, to allow whatever happens to happen. Each person is a free agent, and let's see what they will do. The thinking here is that rather than imposing a structure – or a pattern – on to the session, with Claire giving directions as to what to do when, a more spontaneous pattern may grow from all members of the group. Someone might pick up a drumstick and give a few beats, someone else say 'hmmm… that's nice, do some more', then a few more drum beats and a third person might strum a bit on the guitar. Then they might stop playing, talk a bit, someone will say, 'how does that song go… remember the one…', someone else begins to hum it, and off they go. Claire would be part of the general event. Or she might say, 'let's do that song, I'll play it first and you join in when you are ready'. The two modes of being are very different. In the first scenario, soon the group might create some kind of pattern of being with one another. In the second, Claire would provide a structure, a direction, which enables the group to come together – on her territory or on her terms. And although this might work well – and indeed it does for the particular patients that she describes – the first option is a pattern of relating that demands more responsibility from each member of the group – a responsibility that the patients are not yet ready for. Claire describes them as lacking autonomy and motivation. She needs to be directive, and provide patterns of relating by suggesting musical activities: this gives the group a vocabulary of different ways to be part of a group.

Now let's look at patterns in music.

If we think about patterns in music, then we think about sounds that have sufficient shape for us to hear and know them as music. An endless ongoing sound may have no shape at all – and we stop hearing it after a while. The sounds of a bustling market may have some kind of shape – more like an ongoing hum and erratic punctuation of bicycle bells, a shout here, laughter there. We also stop hearing this after a while. Music has our attention: its patterns engage us. But how?

In group music improvisation, the music needs to be recognizable to more than just the person playing the music. In other words, it must have sufficient predictability, order and space for other members to know when and how to join in. If someone gives a series of regular beats on the drum, then by the third beat, a second person will know when to join in – assuming that they want to play on the same beat. And even if they don't, they still need to know the pattern of the beat in order to play off the beat. So a predictable way of playing allows others to become part of the music making.

However, this predictability also has a difficult side – Claire describes the session in which one person 'played an incessant rhythm for fifty minutes…'. What happens here? His music is predictable and others can join in – but he gets stuck. His playing almost ceases to become music, in the sense that music breathes and moves, but rather, it becomes an alienating stuck pattern; it disables the group. Seaun stops playing, and it is as though this pattern becomes so tightly controlling that there is no space for anyone else to be part of the music. The music belongs to one person only, and this person keeps it that way. The others are not confident or motivated enough to challenge this musical 'hogging'.

In contrast, Claire describes another session in which Seaun takes the initiative – this is quite different to imposing a stuck pattern on the group – and begins 'a strong rhythmic strumming' on the guitar. This invites other members to join in – it is a strumming that they get to know, that is flexible and spacious enough to pull the group together. The others are able to join in easily, playing other instruments, and Seaun becomes the person who supports and holds the group: they need his strumming to keep going. His strumming synthesizes the group – and it may also enable someone to do a 'solo' improvisation above or next to his strumming. For this to happen, Seaun needs to be stable enough to not get 'thrown' by the 'solo' player, and at the same time, he needs to be flexible enough to not restrict the soloist. Indeed, this is what happens in an individual session when Seaun plays the guitar and Claire improvises on the recorder – she is able to do this *because* Seaun has both these qualities: stability and flexibility. Claire describes this as a moment of great intimacy between them.

Finally, we need the forming, un-forming and re-forming of patterns to bring us together in music. We need to create patterns that are not too volatile, or else there will be a feeling of mistrust and unease; and also not too tight or exclusive – because life and relationships have a natural breathing and movement. The sudden stop of Claire's work with Miriam is shocking and brutal: Miriam's emerging trust and healing cannot end naturally, the way that music might end. It is stopped. The pattern is not allowed to complete itself. Music that unfolds, that can be still, that can build up to a tremendous climax, that can be a lilting, gentle trickle or a broad, loud, deep passion – this is the music that reflects and that generates life.

CHAPTER 9

Olive and Jim
Senility and Wisdom[1]

The setting

I remember walking into the Haven and Ethel, this rather wonderful West Indian woman with gorgeous platted grey hair, came up to me and started talking to me. It had all the gestures, all the intonations of talking, but there were no words – she took my hands, looked at me intently and I couldn't understand any of it. It was non-verbal talking. I didn't know what to do, I stood there frozen. Mark, the manager, was with me and he just started to talk with her, to have this conversation with her... he interpreted, and responded to her jumbled words, which he could do. And I remember thinking, 'what am I doing, I haven't the faintest idea where to begin...'.

It took me quite a few weeks to feel that I had any grasp of the client-group in terms of their needs, how I felt about them, how to work with them. I felt intimidated by the fact that they were my grandparents' generation, people with all their wisdom – and who was I to come in and offer anything? I felt inadequate, not ready to take this step. I was so caught up in my personal experience of old people, and my own fears of my own mortality... and I thought, I never want to become senile like this, I never want to be in a home like this, be treated like this.... I never want to lose so much of my life like this. With those negative feelings I

1   Based on the interview with Judith Nockolds. Judith works with adults and children with a complex range of needs, and with elderly people with advanced dementia.

was never going to value the people at the Haven for who they were and how they could be.

I forgot that there is always the music.

The Haven is run by an NHS Trust, and is a forty-five bed residential unit that admits elderly people when community or home care cannot cope anymore. The Haven is their last home: it has a policy of non-resuscitation, and avoids moving people to hospital if at all possible. Most of the residents die there. The atmosphere is generally fairly depressed, the staff are underpaid, and there is a huge turnover of staff because many are in-between jobs and are not skilled workers. They have inadequate training so don't know how to get the best out of their working environments… lack of funding is the bottom line. There are also dedicated, inspiring people.

The building has a central area which is where the music therapy room is, and also the reception area. This is light with lots of windows, and there are three units placed in a circle around the central area. Each unit has fifteen beds, with its own staff, a sitting area, TV and dining room, and each resident has their own bedroom. It attempts not to be clinical but still ends up being that… the philosophy is to provide a more homely environment….

Olive

When I first met Olive I was very struck by her presence. She was a good friend of Ethel's – and they used to walk around arm-in-arm. They were both walkers, Olive was very driven by her walking. She never slept, she catnapped for twenty minutes at a time and generally walked for up to twenty-two hours a day. And if you walked with her you could sort of have a dialogue with her but you had to walk. Any conversation was very much in the here-and-now and never developed beyond that. You could listen to what she said, answer her – there was no flow in the conversation, her flow was very much in her walking. She was a tiny woman, with a shock of white hair, and very beautiful, piercing blue eyes which could really look into you. I always had a feeling of being looked into, by her. There was a liveliness about her – she was eighty, and undeterred by her age. And so much energy!

When I met her she was walking with Ethel, telling her what to do, and Ethel would answer her, very earnestly. Olive would get fed-up with Ethel because Ethel would want to sit down and not walk. They had this rather wonderful relationship... sometimes Ethel would come into the music therapy sessions with Olive and usually sleep – but she'd be there.

Olive would come into the session and become very quickly anxious. If I managed to engage her musically she would stay for a little while, but as soon as that engagement was gone, then she was off – walking. Her aim was to get back home, to see her mother, or else her children would be waiting for her, she had a high level of anxiety. If I tried to distract her, this would just reinforce her anxiety, so I would accept this and say 'well you can come back later'. Sometimes she did come back again for another ten minutes. Music therapy offered Olive a respite from this driven, exhausting walking... I think she walked herself to death; she went very quickly, had a sudden heart attack. At times she'd become very angry: she would see people walking in and out the front door of the Haven, and would become very cross. Because she couldn't.

Olive was very insightful. Her short-term memory was immensely impaired, but in terms of her own situation I think there was a huge amount of insight... and a huge amount of anger and frustration. I saw the walking as a part of her dealing with that: there was a relentlessness about her walking which must have reflected her feelings of having lost so much.

I worked with her for about ten sessions, of varying lengths. I want to play you a bit of one session... so you can hear what she was able to offer, from her situation. You can hear her coming in and beginning to play the drum, and what I heard on the drum was the energy of her walking. And there is also an element of performance: Olive was a performer! There is a feeling of 'I'm going to play the drum' – she was tiny about 4ft 8in! I start to sing and she reflects the harmonies that I'm improvising at the piano, and then starts her own song... we have this rather wonderful improvisation. Olive's voice is strong and lively. It is low, and bristles with energy. The words of her song are: 'I'm forever waiting for the one I really love... never mind... soon go over... come back again... we're fine together... 'bye 'bye my darling ... want to see you soon again...'. You can hear how astonishing her vocal freedom is: her voice has wide contours, she is very free in her singing, with an interweaving of her and my phrases over the pedal point of the music. And the emotional texture of the singing is warm, there is a real feeling of merging between us.

Then she wanted to go! I said 'Oh no, don't go now, it was so lovely, I want to do some more...' so I start singing goodbye – you know the music therapy trick, the elongated goodbye... works perfectly. But on the whole, her preoccupation with walking, and her drivenness, inhibited other possibilities of communication. But listen to the emotional expression in her singing! I think the words were important to her... they were part of her expression – I reflected, I mirrored the words by singing them back to her, letting her lead with them.

The work that I did with Olive validated me. It made me feel I was on the right track, that I had something very real to offer – not just to Olive: I knew that if Olive could access music, then surely the other residents could too. Olive took me away from that feeling of 'what am I doing, is it right, is it appropriate'. And it bridged realities: one of the things I feel about people with senile dementia is that I don't want to ever say or think that my reality is the right one, and that theirs is wrong. This is so denying of that individual! Rather, we need to find a way of being in that person's reality without being condescending, without denying either that reality or the present. Music is a perfect way of doing this because you don't need to get caught up in the words. For example, one of my clients is constantly calling me 'mum'. I can take that into the music, and we have had lovely songs about her mother and she's talked about her mother and has obviously moved from thinking that I am her mother: she has been able to talk about her mother in a more direct and personal way. Bridging those two realities without discounting either one or the other seems to me to be important – and respectful.

I went to fetch Olive for a session one day and they said 'Oh no, Olive's died'. Nobody had told me, nobody prepared me – just like that – gone. I'm glad she went quickly.... Yes, I do form a strong attachment, and we share... but to a certain extent part of me is relieved when someone dies – because I do feel that many of the residents are depressed. There is a theory of 'happy oblivion', but I don't share that idea, and that is not my experience. Maybe it makes it easier for us to bear, not having to face someone else's pain.

But the story I really want to tell you is of the work with Jim.

Jim

When I first met Jim, he was sitting in the centre area of the Haven, so he could watch what was going on. He needed to know what was going on, who was who... and he was aware and alert, although he had a diagnosis of dementia. He'd had a history of ill-health, ending up with a brain tumour and a shunt. His wife says that about ten years ago, at the time of the brain tumour, everything started to go wrong: it sounds to me like there was some sort of brain damage as well.

Jim was such a manly man, and needed to have that manliness reinforced. He was a flirt. One of the staff called him Romeo – and in the nicest way this was right. He needed to be reaffirmed. He was very, very angry at what had happened to him. His wife used to come to the Haven and visit him every morning, and at times he would be aggressive towards her: he was convinced that she was having an affair and would shout at her. She was in her eighties and couldn't cope with him anymore – that was one of the reasons he was in the Haven. He was so negative about himself, about his sexuality, his impotence... he'd been active in the Second World War and had been shot in Japan, he had three medals, and was constantly telling people about his medals – again, you see, reaffirmation about how useful he'd been as a man. He'd been shot in his legs, and although he could walk, he needed a walking frame. His preoccupation was very much that he used to be able to do things... 'and now I'm useless, useless to everyone, I should be dead, what is the point of being alive...'. He spent a lot of time shouting, swearing, and being quite abusive and disruptive.

Jim was eighty-two years old, wore very thick, framed glasses and was balding, so you could see his shunt. He looked frail. When he walked it was a big effort: it would take us about twenty-five minutes to walk to the session, but it was important to him that he got there under his own steam. He would say to me, 'don't you get fed up with waiting for me?' and I would say 'we've lots of time, Jim, don't worry…'.

I gave him a drum and a cymbal at the first session… and I have never heard someone so frail make so much noise! It was as though all of the big manly Jim came out in his drum playing. His beating was quite chaotic, and it was difficult for me, at the piano, to find a way of working with his beat. I'm not sure that I ever succeeded, but after a while I realized that what was important was his emotional discharge: it was to make a big noise, to be a big person. So, rather than to try and frame this drumming, to try and code it into a nice steady beat, what I did with it was to contain his chaotic drumming by improvising some big and holding music, and this allowed him to just really go. He would totally exhaust himself because he wasn't particularly strong… but his need to make a lot of noise was huge, and we did that for quite a few weeks.

He began to develop this fantasy that he was in a band, that he was my drummer and after every session he'd say 'I'm a useless drummer, are you sure you can't find a better drummer?' And I'd say, 'no Jim, I really want to make music with you, you are my drummer!' He'd smile and walk out and say to everyone, 'did you hear me, I am a drummer, I'm really good at the drums' and the next week he'd come back and say 'I've been asked to play in a band!' It was such a positive experience for him to be valued for doing something that felt really important to him. And he'd constantly need affirmation that what he was doing was OK. Through the music, I could validate him. I don't think he heard my validation in words, if you like, but I think he heard it in the music, and he felt it.

He began asking every day, 'Where is Judith! Ring her up!' and get quite angry because I wasn't there – I was only there once a week. So when I got in each week, everyone would say, 'Oh go and see Jim please, he's been asking for you all week!' I'd go and see him and he'd grip my hands and say, 'I'm so glad you're here, I didn't think you were coming, do you want me today, do you want me to do the drumming today?' His wife got drawn in too, because she'd have the experience of seeing him pleased about something, so in a way music therapy became very important for them both.

Sometimes he'd use his voice but generally the session was spent drumming... for twenty to twenty-five minutes. The music that I improvised was big, energetic, it was often in Spanish-type style: this had something to do with the emotional colour that he needed, that his drumming demanded of me. Or at times we would do a big waltz. We would do a lot of *accelerandos* getting louder and louder and faster and faster, building up, and he'd get really excited.... The amount of energy that he put into his drumming was phenomenal, and in some ways, it far exceeded the actual sound that he was able to produce! And I felt that if I could make a big sound too, on the piano, then he could experience his own bigness through that. In some ways I felt frustrated for him because I wanted him to be really able to do this, do the *accelerando* and the build-up in the music – and he couldn't. He was quite limited – but he could still get very excited, and it really felt as though this kind of playing was a big release for him.

At one point I wondered whether I was conning him because I was doing so much of the work. But when I really evaluated what he got from it, I thought no, I'm not – I am helping him to be the big man he needs to be. So much of his verbalizing was about feeling impotent, de-skilled, devalued... as a man. And I felt an enormous amount of empathy for him – and I think he saw me as this young woman who was taking an interest in him. He would say things like, 'they're all jealous because I am in here and they are not' ... that was part of his need to be valued as a man and the music was a vehicle for this.

Then he had a stroke and lost all his movement. He was very, very depressed. He couldn't walk any more, his speech became very blurred, it was difficult to understand what he was trying to say, and I had this gut fear of 'what are we going to do... Jim plays the drums and he can't do that anymore...' I was terrified that I was going to reinforce his sense of loss even more, by bringing him into a situation where he could no longer do what he had been doing. I questioned whether I should.

Mark had rung me up and said Jim had had a stroke and really wasn't very well, so I went to see him and his face absolutely lit up when he saw me. He was so pleased to see me – and I had the realization that the relationship is just as important as the drumming: trust it. We gave it a go, we got him in the wheelchair and I wheeled him along to the music therapy room. And he tried to tell me what had happened ... 'I'm even more useless now'... I listened; listened to the sounds of his talking, the rhythm and phrasing of it as I wheeled him to the piano, and started to play.

What was so amazing... was that he found a way of being big through his voice. Unsolicited by me. He managed to build the sound up and up and up and suddenly he was still this big man in the session, and we worked vocally, and it was so beautiful... just because he was able to find that for himself! And it was so unexpected for me, I didn't trust that he could do that. But he did... here is a recording of our first session after his stroke.

> The piano music on the tape is slow, tender and warm. Judith sings 'hello, Jim, hello Judith...'. Jim joins in. His voice sounds strong and the music is unhurried, restful, in a major key, the music takes its time, it is spacious. And then begins to change. It moves towards more detached playing, with an um-pah, it becomes slightly jazzy with a lift, a bit of a kick and his voice begins to rise... towards long phrases. Then the music becomes stronger, it begins to broaden out towards a point of... something like rock 'n' roll – and he's there, with it, in it... there is no sense of the music pulling or pushing him: his impulse is part of Judith's impulse, and hers is part of him.... 'we can sing a song... together... Yeeeesss! We can sing a song... a song... together!' They play it again, a speeded up version, Jim sings with his entire being – I hear all of him in his voice....

That's right! His voice becomes stronger and stronger, more confident... when I listened back to the tape I though 'oooh, am I imposing on him...' but in some ways it really helped... the music animated him, it enlivened him. And it is a great pleasure and joy to me too! We had a real sense of intimacy... that's the word – I am so aware of doing wonderful music with him, when I am in the middle of it, I get very excited and in it... and it is not me doing it *for* him, it is very much doing it *with* him. I can remember feeling so excited that this was happening, because I'd had such a dread before this session – that I wasn't going to be able to do anything for him... I was so shocked at seeing him, such a physical deterioration, so depressed... and I'd had an inner panic....

He then got to a point where he couldn't come to the music therapy room any longer. I'd go to his bed and sing with him. Well, I sang for him really... he was very weak... and I felt privileged that our music continued right to the very end. This helped me as well: knowing how to be with him when he was coming in and out of consciousness... I'd sit and hold his hand and sing... he showed me how to be with him. It was such a lesson in having faith in what I was doing – it was such a humbling experience because I was so terrified that there'd be nothing more we could do – and actually he showed me....

I was closely involved with his dying because I'd become friends with his wife, and the staff all knew that I was important to him. They told me when they thought he was going to go and I was able to go and say my goodbyes. It was important for me to do that. At his funeral I had such a sense of privilege of having been able to share with him what I shared with him. He was eighty-three when he died, his life had been challenging, and he'd also got a lot out of it. Again I felt a release for him, because he was not happy, being affected by the illness in the way he was....

I miss him. I miss the work with him.

Coda

With this whole client group what I have experienced is contact with that healthy side... with the cohesive side... rather than with the 'affected' side.... I believe that the core of the human being is there and is unaffected – because that is what I am working with: this core of humanity can be contacted in this positive creative way! The rest of the patients' lives is about day to day care and management, and not about communication and not about creativity! And the belief that people with dementia haven't got anything more to offer and there is no more room for growth is absolute nonsense – I know damn well there is!

The music offers a place where the whole of the person can be integrated: yes, Jim was dependent on me bringing him because he couldn't walk... but that didn't matter: the impairment didn't matter. What mattered was what could happen in the music room. I had a belief in – I *expected* something to happen in the music therapy room. And that expectation was so different to his experiences outside the music therapy room! I had expectations of Jim, of the situation, and this by-passed all my knowledge about his impairment, his dependency. The expectation was about me and him in that situation, and the mutuality that could come out of our music.

Sometimes in my work I use old songs – songs that are part of people's younger, earlier lives – as a starting point, but only if we need to. Sometimes using old, familiar songs can be a way of introducing the music room and this is what we can do. Perhaps, though, taking people back to an earlier time of their lives can detract from the here-and-now. And I think so much that the here-and-now has to have value! Life is here, now… it is not what happened forty years ago, it is about now. And even now, with dementia, you can have new experiences, you can be valued for what you can bring to those new experiences… for the gifts you have.

Jim was a great rock'n'roll fan!

Reflections

Music-talk

Ethel talks but has no words. She makes sounds that dive and swell, stop suddenly and accelerate, accompanied by intense gestures and facial expressions. Yes, she is talking, and no, her talking doesn't make sense.

Does it not? Why not? Talking is not only saying words – it is also moving with them, meaning them through the intensity, rhythm, phrasing, loudness or quietness of their sounds. Ethel can make all of those sounds, and can also express herself through the way she walks: restless, energetic, relentless. These tell us something not only about the way she walks, but about her as a person: something about the quality of who she is. In her work with Olive, Judith hears the same energy in Olive's drumming as she sees in her walking. This tells us that the quality of who we are expresses itself in how we talk, how we move, how we gesture, how our face looks and moves… and often the music therapist 'tunes into' this essential quality of a person not so much by their music-making (especially if they refuse to play), but through the quality of their movements, gestures, facial expressions – and through the sounds that they make. Judith 'knows' Olive, even though they have not had a verbal conversation by the time she comes to music therapy. The chances are that if Olive's walking bristles with energy, then so will her talking, her movements, the way that she expresses her irritation and anxiety. And the way she beats the drum. Olive can make music, and music does not need words.

There is a complication, however. Unlike Ethel, Olive *has* words – but they don't always 'make sense'. Some of the things she says (e.g. her mother waiting for her, she needs to see her mother) are inaccurate, since her mother is long gone. On the other hand, if we use our imagination, she may indeed be seeing her mother and experiencing her as waiting for her... on the 'other side'. Olive has insight – it is not necessarily a 'logical' or a 'verbal' insight: rather, she has a sense of being cooped up in this place, of wanting to get out, and of being frustrated and unhappy because she cannot. And most likely, a lot of other insights as well that we cannot quite access through words.

Jim's insight is clearer and more accessible to us: he feels useless, does Judith really want him to come and drum for her? And oooh, what a lovely young woman she is. It would seem, then, that each of the three, Olive, Ethel and Jim, know their condition – have insight into it.

In the music therapy sessions with Olive and with Jim, Judith is able to create the most beautiful, tender music. With Olive, the music has astonishing emotional freedom, and her singing bristles with energy: this tiny, unhappy woman who spends all day walking and talking with someone who has no words, her friend Ethel! In music therapy she unfolds herself to her full emotional stature: Olive is fully alive, in the minutes that she manages to spend in the music therapy room, before resuming her relentless walking.

Jim manages to be a big man – possibly the big man he has never been – despite his frailties and, eventually, his stroke. The music respects his bigness, evokes it, invites it – and addresses his healthy, emotional aliveness. Jim sings with his heart and soul! He can be part of Judith's playing, which is ready to expand with him, which can be tender, inviting, highly energetic, and even challenging, urging him on towards stronger, larger music. Although his beating is chaotic, which means that Judith cannot always 'meet' it and play with him in his beat, the range and colour and depth of her music allows him to 'let go'. He can release his enormous emotional energy, and the piano music can 'hold' his 'big noise'. It does not swallow him up by being bigger than he is, while also not leaving him to be 'big' and 'noisy' alone. Judith is right there, with him in the music. And the music colours his 'inner being' – not the Jim who is frail and struggles to get to the music room in under twenty minutes, but the Jim who fought wars, was decorated; the Jim who is potent.

Throughout this story, Judith shares her own vulnerabilities and uncertainties. When she first arrives at the Haven, she is filled with a sense of her own mortality. She isn't sure whether she can work with people who have dementia. She describes working with Olive as validating her, allaying her anxieties about whether she can do this work. And her work with Jim she describes as a privilege; as him having shown her what he needed from her. These two elderly people enter a journey with Judith, and she with them: this is a mutual journeying, for both the therapist and the patients, and this mutuality happens because they meet one another at the level of our essential humanity. Dementia may mean that our 'reason' and 'logic' and 'talking' are dented – but essentially, we remain who and how we are – just as Judith, the music therapist, is Judith the human being. In the sessions she is not only the music therapist, doing her 'work'. The *whole* of herself is involved: she is in a panic when Jim has had a stroke – this is a *personal* feeling, that she cannot ignore or push aside as not being part of her professional identity. And although she does not share her panic with Jim, she acknowledges her feelings of panic *to herself.* And when Olive sings beautifully, Judith is excited, the music is so wonderful. It is not only Olive who enjoys herself in music therapy!

There is also a sense, in this story, that Judith is not working with 'patients' – people who have dementia – but rather, with integrated human beings, with Olive and Jim, in all their frailty and strength, illness and health. With their senility and their wisdom.

Conclusion
Intimate Notes

If it has no science, it fails;
if it has no craft, it bores;
if it has not art, it offends.

(Source unknown)

Music therapy invites the art, science and craft of music and healing. Illness, disease and disablement are not simply scientifically significant conditions needing 'treatment' or 'cure'. They are conditions that allow richness and meaning into our lives, demanding to be heard, expressed, re-created and given inspiration.

The science of economics, however, has another dynamic. Many of us practise in contexts that demand 'facts and figures', 'proof' that music therapy 'works', and tangible, quantifiable 'results'. We find ourselves in a complex situation. We could, if we wanted and needed to, assess the benefits of music therapy by measuring observable changes in each of the clients in these stories, comparing their 'behaviour' before and after 'treatment', for example. We could also do micro-analyses of musical developments and musical responses over a series of sessions. And indeed, we do analyse and measure when and if employers or research projects demand it. Some music therapy journals are full of such studies, both qualitative and quantitative, and these make a strong case for the efficacy of our work.

But to be satisfied with just the 'science of success' is limiting. The artist and the artisan in each of us demand much more than 'success' and 'progress'. There are complex and multi-layered meanings in music therapy – verbal, musical and neither of these – that we need to unfold without being too conclusive, in order to enrich our insights into the work. The richer and more complex our understandings and insights, the richer the experiences we are able to share with clients. This richness of meaning allows the artistry in all of our lives – whatever our limitations, disabilities, diseases and needs – to be evoked in music therapy.

We have seen that the use of music as a therapeutic and relational event allows an interplay between our emotional and physical lives. When we sing or play, we sound ourselves: how we feel, how we are at that moment, how we relate with another person and come to experience ourselves directly within that relationship. Throughout these stories there is a sense of music therapists not protecting themselves from their *own* feelings about clients. In our interviews, none of the music therapists hid their feelings: they spoke of fears, anxieties, frustrations, love, sadness, joy, despair, and did not leave aside their 'personhood', while being professional. Being in music with clients, and invoking and accompanying their images, demands the whole of our self. We cannot leave this aside in sessions.

However, the music therapist's skill lies in not becoming *overwhelmed* by personal feelings in sessions: it would not help the client to have the therapist dissolve into tears or give vent to frustration. Rather, by *feeling* those feelings, and by being able to contain them, music therapists allow themselves to be open and responsive to the other person.

The music is the centre point. Through listening to music, as in the GIM session, Martha is journeyed to a latent world of her own images, waiting to be triggered into her conscious daily life. Through making sounds with their voices, Daniel, Shireen, Giorgos and Sinead reveal an intimate, invisible part of themselves: a part that each therapist instantly recognizes and acknowledges as focal. Something about each of them is unfolded, through their voice; called forth, evoked towards an extension of themselves, towards a fuller living.

The 'pathology' of clients fades in these stories. In listening to Judith and Jim, we hear not only Jim's disablement – particularly after his severe stroke – we hear also his strength, his potency, vigour and energy. These remain with him, are an essential part of him – a part that we

CONCLUSION   143

might well miss and forget, were we to only focus on his 'behaviour' before and after music therapy. Wendy ceases to be only a tormented, unhappy child, and becomes transformed, through singing, dancing, playing, into a powerhouse of passion, free expressiveness and creativity: she is extended towards her full human potential, and soon, the changes in the music therapy sessions transfer into other areas of her life. She is able to concentrate and learn at school, and is discharged from the hospital into an ordinary school.

In the group music therapy sessions in the secure unit, various people – all offenders – are given the opportunity to be with one another in an expressive, creative, and less structured way. The absence of a 'set' structure or formula for group sessions is threatening to the group members: they need Claire to be 'directive'; to give them the vocabulary of existing possibilities, so that they might begin to develop their interactive and expressive skills with one another, through music.

In music improvisation between a therapist and patient/client, there are no 'right' and 'wrong' notes: all are part of possibility. Steve's complex drumming is not simply chaotic: it possesses the possibility of rhythmic freedom and complexity, reflecting and presenting the richness of his essential self. Possibility itself gives suffering and celebration a voice. This voice – this music – is unique to that person and the music therapist in relation to one another. They need one another in order to imagine, and render the world anew; and in order to activate the inherent capacity to heal which is present in all persons. In this sense, healing is not necessarily 'getting better' or being 'cured' from dementia or disability or HIV/AIDS. Rather, healing is the authentic voicing of who we fully are, in a way that discards the passivity and smallness of being *only* disabled, *only* ill and *only* disturbed.

This book opened with Oksana alluding to the spirituality of the work. Some music therapists speak of it directly, others imply it tacitly. A few of the stories make no reference to it at all – and the literature on music therapy, with very few exceptions, ignores this dimension. And yet, at this profoundly personal and interpersonal level of being, and of giving voice to the creativity (and suffering) of one's life, the depth and breadth of life and music challenge boundaries of secular reality and knowledge. In this sense, the use of improvisation in music therapy is a metaphor for the unexpectedness of life. This includes a spiritual reality, one that has no public or collective dogma, and that cannot begin to be adequately portrayed by words alone.

Music quickens the spirit, it animates us, moves us towards transcendence and transformation. At the same time, music draws us inwards towards a space of stillness, where all is one. The great Sufi master, Hazrat Inayat Khan, reminds us that music touches our innermost being, and produces new life. This new life gives exaltation to the whole of ourselves, moving us towards that perfection which is oneness.

Further Reading

Aigen, Kenneth (1998) *Paths of Development in Nordoff-Robbins Music Therapy.* Gilsum: Barcelona Publishers.

Aldridge, David (1996) *Music Therapy Research and Practice in Medicine: From Out of the Silence.* London: Jessica Kingsley Publishers.

Ansdell, Gary (1995) *Music for Life.* London: Jessica Kingsley Publishers.

Bruscia, Ken (ed) (1991) *Case Studies in Music Therapy.* Phoenixville, PA: Barcelona.

Bunt, Leslie (1994) *Music Therapy: An Art Beyond Words.* London: Routledge.

Bush, Carol A. (1995) *Healing Imagery and Music, Pathways to the Inner Self. Healing with Sound and Music Series.* Portland, OR: Rudra Press.

Lee, Colin (ed) (1994) *Lonely Waters. Proceedings of the International Conference, Music Therapy in Palliative Care.* Oxford: Sobell House.

Lee, Colin (1996) *Music at the Edge: The Music Therapy Experiences of a Musician with AIDS.* London: Routledge.

Nordoff, Paul and Robbins, Clive (1971) *Therapy in Music for the Handicapped Child.* London: Gollancz.

Nordoff, Paul and Robbins, Clive (1977) *Creative Music Therapy.* New York: John Day.

Pavlicevic, Mercédès (1997) *Music Therapy in Context.* London: Jessica Kingsley Publishers.

Priestey, Mary (1975) *Analytical Music Therapy.* London: Constable.

Streeter, Elaine (1993) *Making Music with the Young Handicapped Child: A Guide for Parents.* London: Jessica Kingsley Publishers.